PRAISE FOR

THE MAKING OF AMERICA
ALEXANDER HAMILTON

"The strength of the book is the generous use of Hamilton's own words . . . A solid introduction to a charismatic founding father."

—Kirkus Reviews

"Thoroughly researched and cited, this book is accessibly written and full of valuable information . . . Hamilton's intelligence, ceaseless drive, and penchant for speaking his mind come across, giving readers a clear view of Hamilton's character and his role in creating America."

—Booklist

"Kanefield is a capable nonfiction writer, organizing an eloquent review of Hamilton's life while balancing the perspectives of his adversaries and skeptics . . . the story is told easily, making a founding father accessible to young readers the way Lin-Manuel Miranda has done on Broadway."

***—Voice of Youth Advocates* (*VOYA*)**

There is properly no history, only biography.
—Ralph Waldo Emerson

★ ★ ★ ★ ★ ★ ★ ★ ★ ★ ★ ★ ★ ★ ★ ★ ★

The Making of America series traces the constitutional history of the United States through overlapping biographies of American men and women. The debates that raged when our nation was founded have been argued ever since: *How should the Constitution be interpreted? What is the meaning, and where are the limits, of personal liberty? What is the proper role of the federal government? Who should be included in "we the people"?* Each biography in the series tells the story of an American leader who helped shape the United States of today.

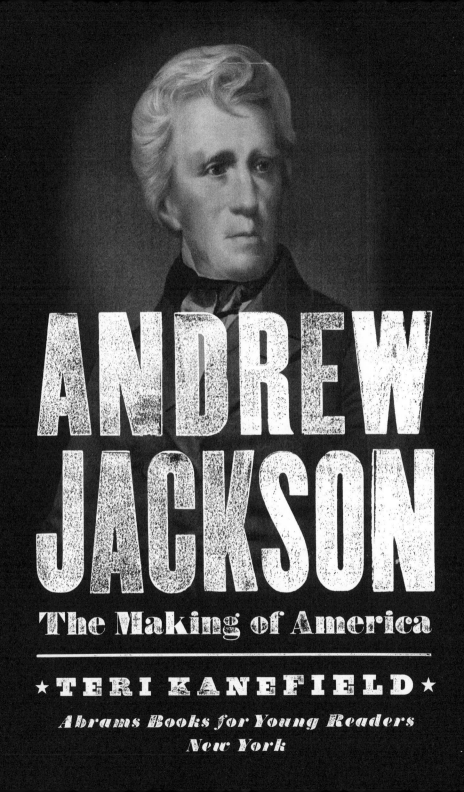

ANDREW JACKSON

The Making of America

★ TERI KANEFIELD ★

Abrams Books for Young Readers
New York

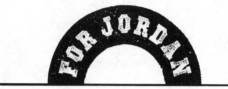

FOR JORDAN

★ ★ ★ ★ ★ ★ ★ ★ ★

All images used in this book are public domain.

Cataloging-in-Publication Data has been applied for
and may be obtained from the Library of Congress.

ISBN 978-1-4197-2840-2

Book design by Sara Corbett

Published in 2018 by Abrams Books for Young Readers, an imprint of ABRAMS.

Printed and bound in U.S.A.
10 9 8 7 6 5 4 3 2 1

ABRAMS The Art of Books
195 Broadway, New York, NY 10007
abramsbooks.com

CONTENTS

★ PROLOGUE ★

A Mob in the White House

On a mild March day in 1829, Andrew Jackson stepped onto the East Portico of the Capitol Building to take the oath of office. He was lanky and tall and sixty-one years old. His hair had long since turned gray, but his piercing blue eyes still radiated strength and vitality. He carried two bullets lodged in his body, one in his chest near his heart and the other in his arm—the remnants of frontier

Jackson's inauguration, 1829. *President's Levee,* also called, *All Creation Going to the White House,* was created by Robert Cruickshank as an illustration in the Playfair Papers, London, 1841.

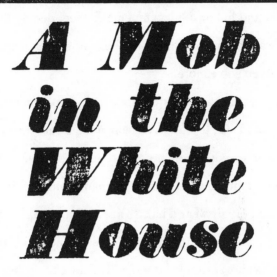

gunfights and his own hot temper. His face, deeply lined with sorrow, was the face of a man who had suffered and triumphed, then suffered some more.

A crowd of more than fifteen thousand people converged upon Washington, D.C., to watch Jackson, a man from the backcountry with limited education, become America's seventh president. Some of his admirers had traveled as many as five hundred miles.

Jackson didn't wear a hat. It was a symbolic gesture showing that he was a servant of the people and not their ruler. His speech was short, simple, and direct. Addressing the crowd as "Fellow citizens," he humbly noted that he was the "choice of a free people" and stated his theory of government: "As long as our government is administered for the good of the people, and is regulated by their will . . . it will be worth defending."

Supreme Court Chief Justice John Marshall held out the Bible. Jackson placed his hand upon it and repeated the oath of office. He then kissed the Bible. Cannon thundered a salute, echoed by gunfire from the Navy Yard.

The rope holding the spectators back was snapped aside, and the crowd lunged forward. Fearing for the new president's safety, his team whisked him into a nearby carriage and headed down Pennsylvania Avenue toward the White House.

A crowd followed. According to custom, new presidents held a private reception at the White House, greeting guests and serving refreshments. Well-wishers were invited to shake the new president's hand. Defying custom, Jackson opened the doors to the public. Members of the crowd, eager to see their hero, swarmed into the White House.

The White House staff set out tables with bread, roast chicken, cakes, and orange punch laced with whiskey. "But what a scene did we witness!" cried Margaret Bayard Smith, a well-to-do Washington society figure. "The majesty of the people had disappeared, and a rabble, a mob, of boys, negroes, women, children, scrambling, fighting, romping. What a pity what a pity!" Another attendee reported that the crowd included "the most vulgar and gross in the nation."

Eager to get a glimpse of their hero, Jackson's admirers stood on furniture, the mud from their boots smearing the damask-covered chairs. The jostling crowds helped themselves to food and punch. A table was knocked over. Glassware crashed to the floor. Punch spilled on the carpet. People wishing to shake Jackson's hand crowded him, pinning him to the wall. Again fearing for his safety, a few men formed a human shield to protect him and helped him flee through a side door to the nearby Gadsby's

Hotel, where he spent the first night of his presidency. Antoine Michel Giusta, the White House steward, induced the crowds outside by moving the punch to the lawn.

For Jackson's admirers, he embodied the true spirit of America—a rugged individualist, a fiercely patriotic war hero, and a frontiersman. To Jackson's enemies, he was a lawless ruffian, a killer, and would-be tyrant. They believed that the chaotic scene at the White House was an omen of what was to come, and they feared that his inauguration would be the start of mob rule in America.

1

A Brutal Boyhood

"It is very true, that early in life, even in the days of my boyhood, I contributed my mite to shake off the yoke of tyranny, and to build up the fabrick of free government."

—Andrew Jackson

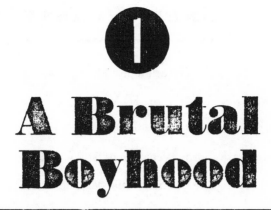

Andrew Jackson grew up on a small farm amid gently rolling hills and dense forests of hickory, oak, and pine. Deer and small game were plentiful enough that, if necessary, a family could survive by hunting. The region, called the Waxhaws, was located directly on the border between the Carolinas. Some farms were in North Carolina and others in South Carolina, but the settlers, mostly new immigrants from Ireland, didn't care which colony their home was in. The only government authority they recognized was the Waxhaws Presbyterian church, and the only laws they followed were derived from the Bible.

Andrew Jackson's father died on March 1, 1767, two weeks before Andrew was born. According to family tradition, Andrew's father died in a logging accident while performing the backbreaking work of carving a farm out of the wilderness. His widow, Betty Jackson, was left to care for newborn Andrew and two older children, Robert, who was then about two, and Hugh, about four. Betty was a stout, no-nonsense woman with flaming red hair and deep blue eyes. She was a tireless worker, but she was unable to

Artist rendition of Andrew Jackson's birthplace. From *Lance, Cross, and Canoe*, by W. H. Milburn, 1893.

manage her farm by herself, so Betty and her boys went to live with one of Betty's sisters, Jane, and her husband, James Crawford. The Crawfords, who had four sons and three daughters,

lived in a farmhouse consisting of one or two downstairs rooms with a loft. Jane was often sick, so Betty managed the household by baking and preparing meals, spinning thread and making clothing, tending gardens—and caring for all ten children.

The Jacksons had immigrated from Ulster, Ireland, the year before Andrew was born. Betty's sisters had come a few years earlier. To escape poverty in Ireland and oppression at the hands of the British, it was common for extended families—and sometimes entire villages—to immigrate together, lured to the Carolinas by promises of rich, fertile land. The Southern colonies encouraged Irish immigration because they wanted to increase the white population: In the event of a slave uprising, they wanted more people fighting on the side of the whites. The Irish, hearty and rugged, adapted easily to the Carolina backcountry. The more established colonists from England scoffed at the Irish immigrants of the Waxhaws, who one traveling Episcopalian minister referred to as "a set of the most lowest vilest crew breathing."

As a young boy, Andrew would have seen slave traders marching captive men and women up the post road that led past the Waxhaws district to be sold in Charlotte, North Carolina. Many in his deeply religious community found justification for slavery in the Bible, where it was commonplace.

Andrew attended school sporadically in a one-room schoolhouse, where he learned reading, writing, arithmetic, and some Latin. He didn't care much for studying and he never learned to spell properly. Later he joked that it was a "poor mind indeed which can't think of at least two ways to spell a word." One historian quipped that Jackson was fully capable of spelling a word four different ways on the same page. Jackson may not have been much of a writer, but he had such a gift for speaking expressively and forcefully that Betty thought he should become a minister. Andrew, however, showed no signs of being destined for the church. He was wild and reckless, jumping fences, playing practical jokes, and frightening people with bloodcurdling oaths. He was also a fighter. When the boys wrestled, Andrew, the youngest, often ended up on the ground, but—in the words of one of his childhood friends—"I could throw him three times out of four, but he would never *stay throwed.* He was dead game, even then, and never would give up."

One day when Andrew was about eight, a group of mischievous boys gave him a shotgun, loaded to the muzzle with powder. They goaded him into firing the gun. When he did, the recoil sent him sprawling to the ground. Furious, he jumped to his feet and said, "By God, if any of you laughs, I'll kill him." Nobody laughed.

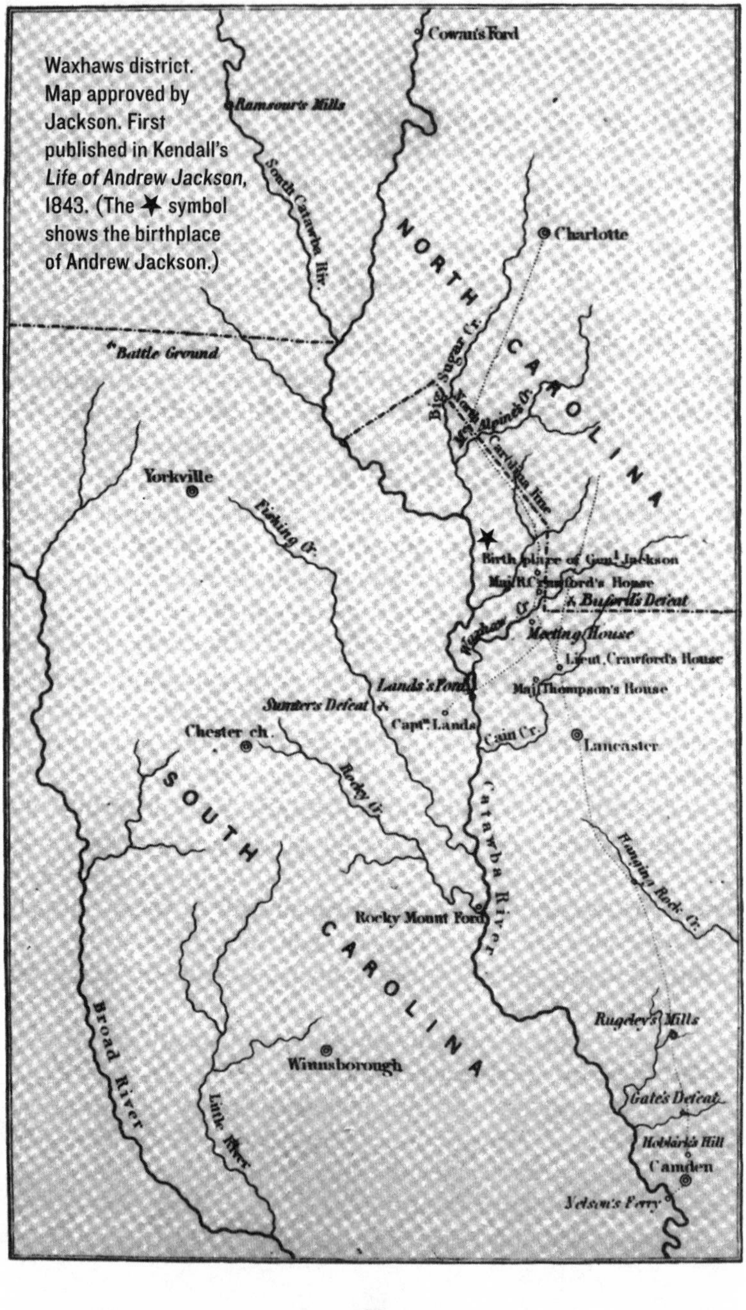

Waxhaws district. Map approved by Jackson. First published in Kendall's *Life of Andrew Jackson*, 1843. (The ★ symbol shows the birthplace of Andrew Jackson.)

Andrew was eight years old when the Revolutionary War broke out, and nine in 1776 when America declared independence from Britain. His family were among those who cheered American defiance. Andrew had already learned to hate the British. Often during long winter evenings by the light of the fire, Betty regaled the youngsters with horrifying stories of how her own father had suffered at the hands of the conquering British, who had treated Irish laboring poor with cruelty and disdain.

Waxhaws men formed a militia and drilled. Even though Andrew was too young to fight, Betty allowed him to join the drills. While the Irish immigrants of the Waxhaws were passionately anti-British, many of those in the surrounding areas remained loyal to the king. Bloody fights broke out between Loyalists, who wanted the colonies to remain part of Britain, and Patriots, who wanted independence. The result was akin to a civil war, with Carolina men often killing one another. One Waxhaws resident later said the Patriots were forced to defend themselves "from the ferocious attacks" of their Loyalist neighbors. One Patriot, after finding a friend murdered and mutilated by a Loyalist, became unhinged, swore revenge on all Loyalists, and scoured the countryside, shooting Loyalists on sight. By the end of the war, he had killed twenty men in cold blood.

For years, the fighting was sporadic, rarely coming close to the Waxhaws. Once, though, fearing an invasion, the Waxhaws men loaded their guns and rode off to repel British attacks. Betty and other women in the family fled with the children to a settlement farther north in North Carolina and took refuge with family there. They remained for several months. Then, in 1779, the entire region braced again for an attack: British forces had taken much of what later became the state of Georgia and were preparing to invade South Carolina. Andrew's brother Hugh secured Betty's permission to join a local militia.

For several weeks, the Crawfords and Jacksons anxiously awaited news of the fighting. First they were buoyed by the encouraging rumor that the British were retreating. Then came news of a devastating defeat at a place called Stono Ferry. They learned that the captain of the South Carolina militia was dead, and Hugh Jackson was dying. Because he'd been sick, the captain ordered him to stay out of the battle, but he fought anyway and collapsed from heat and exhaustion. He made it home, but died soon after arriving. His family, distraught, consoled themselves with the thought that he'd died in a noble cause—fighting the British for American independence.

Not long afterward, the British attacked a band of Patriot

soldiers in the vicinity of the Waxhaws. The wounded were carried to the Waxhaws meeting house, which was hastily converted into a hospital, with straw spread on the floor to soak up the blood. Andrew and his mother helped tend the injured. There wasn't much they could do other than bandage wounds and offer whiskey to dull the pain. Because the bodies of many of the killed and wounded were badly mangled with multiple wounds—some had limbs cut off—the attack was called a massacre and the British commander, Lieutenant-Colonel Banastre Tarlteton, a butcher.

It was Andrew's first close-up look at the horrors of war. Later he recalled that none of the wounded had fewer than four gaping wounds. Some had as many as thirteen. The sight angered and hardened him. Not long after the massacre, as Andrew later recalled, Tarleton himself "passed through the Waxhaws, passing our dwelling but all were *hid out.* Tarleton passed within a hundred yards of where I & a cousin crawford, had concealed ourselves. I could have shot him."

Andrew longed to join the fighting. Betty forbid it because he was still too young, but she allowed him and his brother Robert to accompany Patriot soldiers on several expeditions. Andrew's task, as a boy of thirteen, was to carry messages and tend to the soldiers. On one excursion, Andrew and Robert accompanied about five hundred men to Stokes County, North Carolina. Many of the soldiers had very little ammunition—some had only one or two bullets. Others had no guns at all. Their only hope was to take the British by surprise. Those without guns planned to wait behind. If any British soldiers ran away, they would try to grab their muskets so they could get into the fight.

The British were camped in the woods along the road not far from the well-known landmark of an enormous jutting rock called Hanging Rock. When the men set out for the raid, Andrew hid in a wooded ravine, from where he was able to watch much of the battle.

The Battle of Hanging Rock was bloody and lasted hours in blistering August heat. During a lull, the Americans were able to loot the British camp of all clothing, guns, and valuables—including rum, which the Americans used to quench their thirst. A group of British reinforcements arrived, so the weary—and somewhat intoxicated—Americans retreated. It was later said that the Americans would have won the battle had the soldiers not dipped into the rum.

★ ★ ★ ★ ★ ★ ★ ★ ★ ★ ★ ★ ★ ★ ★

When Andrew turned fourteen, Betty allowed him to fight as a soldier. One night, he was staying in the home of John Land, the captain of a local militia, when he heard someone outside. It was late, and the fire had burned low. Andrew and another soldier staying in the house crept outside. Andrew released the catch on his musket and prepared to fire. To the right, near the corn crib, were shadows that could have been a large group of men. He rested his musket in the fork of an apple tree, having learned his lesson about the recoil. "Who goes there?" he shouted.

Battle of Hanging Rock. *Attack on Hollow Square at Hanging Rock*, artist unknown, circa 1900.

Nobody answered. He squeezed the trigger. Whoever was in the corn crib fired back, killing the man by Andrew's side. Andrew scooted back into the cabin. From the window he saw the attackers coming toward the house. His uncle and brother, awakened by the gunfire, joined him at one of the doors. Andrew reloaded, stuffed a few bullets into his mouth for convenient reloading, and waited. He knew the men in the house were outnumbered, but he intended to fight to the last. Suddenly, the attackers turned and left. Andrew never knew what saved their lives.

★ ★ ★ ★ ★ ★ ★ ★ ★ ★ ★ ★ ★ ★ ★

One morning, both Robert and Andrew were in the home of an uncle, Thomas Crawford, with Betty and a few young cousins when there came the clatter of hoofs in the yard outside. Betty ran to the door. A group of British soldiers burst into the cabin. The soldiers forced all the inhabitants into a corner and plundered the house, looking for valuables, overturning furniture and ripping clothing. Later the family learned that a Loyalist had directed the British to their home.

The officer in command ordered Andrew to clean his

mud-covered boots. Andrew refused, saying, "I am a prisoner of war and claim to be treated as such." He spoke with characteristic boldness. He was also making a political point. The British treated the American Patriots as rebels and criminals. The Americans viewed themselves as soldiers fighting a war.

The officer, enraged, lifted his sword and aimed it directly at Andrew's head. Andrew ducked and raised his left hand in time to break the full force of the blow. The blow might have killed him. Instead, it gave him a deep gash on the head and sliced into his hand. He fell to the floor, in pain, bleeding profusely. He carried the scar from that blow for the rest of his life.

The officer then ordered Robert to clean his boots. When Robert, too, refused, the officer hit him so hard with his sword that he went sprawling across the room.

The officers burned the house to the ground and took both boys and one of their cousins prisoner. Determined to root out every rebel in the area, the British ordered Andrew to guide them to the home of Tommy Thompson, who they knew to be a rebel. Andrew complied with the orders, but he chose a route that allowed Thompson to see them approach, giving him enough time to escape across the creek with his horse.

Later that day, Andrew, Robert, one of their cousins, and a

few others were taken by horseback to Camden—a village forty miles away. For the injured boys, it was a long and painful ride. In Camden, they were brought to the jail—a heavily fortified building used for horse thieves. Later Andrew described what happened after he, his brother, and cousin were brought to the prison:

> As soon as our relationship was known, we were separated from each other. No attention whatever was paid to the wounds or to the comfort of the prisoners, and the smallpox having broken out among them, for the want of proper care, many fell victims to it. I frequently heard them groaning in the agonies of death and no regard was paid to them.

After two excruciating weeks in the prison, Andrew looked through the window and saw an American soldier appearing in the distance. Andrew supposed he was a deserter. The arrival of the soldier caused a stir among the British. At sunset, British soldiers came and nailed planks across the window of Jackson's cell. The soldier told the prisoners they would all soon be hanged. The prisoners knew from the stirring of British troops that something was about to happen. Andrew later described how he chiseled a peephole in the planks:

> Being anxious to see the battle if one took place, having only a razor blade which was allowed us to divide our rations with, I fell to work to cut out a pine knot out of the plank nailed over the windows . . . and with the aid of a fellow prisoner, completed my object before day, making an aperture about an inch in diameter.

From this peephole, Andrew and the other prisoners took turns watching the fight that was later called the Battle of Hobkirk's Hill. They watched the British burst from the woods to attack. The Americans, though surprised, rallied quickly. Cannon boomed. Swords flashed. Later Andrew wrote—with his usual rhetorical flair and errors in English usage: "Never were hearts elated more than ours at the glitter of the americans swords." Before long, though, came crushing disappointment: Andrew and the others took turns at the peephole, watching as the Americans retreated.

The following day, Andrew's mother arrived at the jail with Jane Walker, another Waxhaws woman. Jane's brother, a Patriot captain, had captured thirteen British soldiers. Jane arranged a prisoner exchange—the British soldiers for seven Waxhaws soldiers, including Andrew and Robert.

Once the boys were released, Robert, Andrew, and Betty set out for home. They had only two horses. Robert was so sick that he had to be strapped onto his horse. Andrew was strong enough to walk the entire forty-five miles, so his mother rode the other horse. The British had taken Andrew's shoes and jacket, so he walked the entire way cold and barefoot. As Andrew himself later described the last part of the journey, "The fury of a violent storm of rain to which we were exposed for several hours before we reached the end of our journey caused the smallpox to strike in and consequently the next day I was dangerously ill."

In fact, both Andrew and Robert came down with the deadly smallpox. Upon arriving home, both boys took to their beds. Painful sores flared on their mouths and throats, followed by splitting headaches, nausea, fever, and delirium. Andrew, deathly ill, later described himself as a raving maniac. Robert died of the illness. Many months passed before Andrew found himself on the way to recovery. Eventually the painful sores subsided and he regained his strength.

* * * * * * * * * * * * * * *

Meanwhile, fighting raged in South Carolina. About the time Andrew recovered from smallpox, the residents of Waxhaws learned that another prisoner exchange was being arranged in Charles Town, now called Charleston. Among those captured were two of Andrew's cousins, William and Jas Crawford, who were imprisoned on a ship. His mother and aunt made plans to set off for Charleston, 160 miles away, to bring the boys back. To get to Charleston, they would have to travel through pine forests, marshes, and sandy fields scattered with the ruins of war—half-burnt houses, crumbling chimneys, and desolation. The journey would take four days, or longer if the rivers were high.

Both Betty and Andrew understood the dangers of the journey. Given the rampant and highly contagious diseases among those imprisoned on ships, it was possible she might never return. Her final words to Andrew were, "Make friends by being honest. Keep them by being steadfast. Andy, never tell a lie or take what is not yours." She added a curious bit of advice: "Never sue for slander. Settle them cases yourself." With the clairvoyance of a mother, she must have known that her thin-skinned son—who had a temper and a tendency to misbehave—would spend his life defending his reputation.

A few weeks later, the prisoners returned, but Betty wasn't with them. She had died of a fever she'd picked up while caring for sick men from the prisons. Her death devastated Andrew. Later he tried in vain to locate the place of her death and burial.

A few months after Betty Jackson died, British General Cornwallis surrendered after the Siege of Yorktown. Cornwallis's crushing defeat rendered the British ready to negotiate peace. For more than a year, the British continued to occupy South Carolina, but the fighting ended.

The Revolutionary War had taken both of Andrew's brothers and his mother, leaving him an orphan at the age of fourteen. For many of the Founding Fathers—elite, well-educated, and deeply-versed in history and the classics—the American Revolution was an ideal born in the library and drawing room. The founders envisioned a republic based on the principles of English philosopher John Locke, who had first suggested that a three-part government would allow for checks and balances. The founders declared independence and undertook what they thought of as the great American experiment, defined this way: With a full understanding of human imperfections and the tendency for those in power to abuse it, could the people govern themselves?

For Andrew Jackson, the Revolutionary War was intensely personal. There was nothing intellectual or academic about it. For him, the fight for independence wasn't about reaching for lofty ideals—it was about beating the hated British who had persecuted his family for generations. It was about making ordinary Americans secure in their homes. It was about achieving personal freedom and dignity.

2

Head of All the Rowdies

"[B]rought up under the tyranny of Britain—
altho young embarked in the struggle for our liberties,
in which I lost every thing that was dear to me,
my brothers and my fortune—for which I have
been amply repaid by living under the mild
administration of a republican government."

—Andrew Jackson

After Betty's death, Jackson went to live with an uncle, Robert Crawford—but the arrangement didn't last long. Devastated over the loss of his mother, he was sullen and angry, and soon got into a quarrel with a houseguest named Captain Galbraith. When the captain took offense at something Jackson said and raised his hand as if to slap him, Jackson exploded in a rage. He swore that if Galbraith laid a hand on him, Galbraith would be a dead man. Galbraith backed off, but a short while later, Jackson packed up and went to live with other relatives, Joseph and Elizabeth White and their four grown sons.

The Whites' farm, nestled in hills between two creeks, was so prosperous that the Whites owned a full set of carpenter's tools and a loom. Two of the sons had learned the art of saddling during the war and were teaching it to their brothers. The work of a saddler appealed to Jackson, who had a passion for horses. He worked in the Whites' saddler's shop as an apprentice in exchange for room and board. He liked the work, and he enjoyed spending time with the White boys, particularly Hugh, who was closest to him in age. After working all day in the saddle shop, Jackson and Hugh often raced horses or went fishing. Hugh was an avid reader and had a large vocabulary, but Jackson had no interest in books. He much preferred drinking, gambling, cockfighting, and raccoon hunting.

At the age of seventeen, Jackson got his first taste of a large city when he made two separate trips to Charleston. Until then, the largest town he'd ever seen was Camden, with a population of about four hundred. Charleston had a whopping fifteen thousand inhabitants, five grand church steeples, fine carriages, large marketplaces, rows of brick buildings, and a real racetrack.

Being from the backcountry, Jackson was what the Charleston gentry referred to as a cracker. He observed the way gentlemen dressed and their manners. He learned about dueling, a ritualized custom among gentlemen. In the backcountry, men frequently settled their differences with fistfights. Among the Charleston well-to-do, a man who felt wronged issued a formally worded challenge. Sometimes the duelers put on a show, agreeing to fire into the air to save face. But often they shot to kill.

A piece of folklore about Andrew Jackson is that he traveled to Charleston to collect a large inheritance from his grandfather in Ireland, which he irresponsibly squandered on gambling and drinking. Then—according to this story—he realized he had to mend his ways and reform. In fact, there is no evidence to back up this account other than a witness who said that Jackson, like "many other such men . . . spent money rather too freely."

Most likely what happened, according to historian Hendrik Booream, was that Jackson came into a small inheritance, which he retrieved in Charleston. The inheritance would explain how he suddenly became the owner of a fine mare.

Jackson stayed in Charleston for a while, then abruptly returned to the Waxhaws with his mind made up: He would improve his station in life by becoming a lawyer, one of the few ways a man from the lower classes could rise into the gentry. A lawyer's work was non-menial, respected, and came with the title of esquire. Besides, there was a shortage of lawyers. Before the war, many lawyers had been Loyalists who had since left to live in England or Canada.

In South Carolina at the time, there was no educational requirement for becoming a lawyer, nor was there a written test. The applicant simply needed to pass an oral examination administered by a local judge. The exam covered basic legal terms and

A section of Charleston, South Carolina, 1800

procedures. To get the necessary training, an aspiring lawyer worked alongside a practicing attorney as an apprentice. The practice of law in backcountry courts was often fairly straightforward. A lawyer had to know how to handle such tasks as interviewing witnesses, gathering evidence for cases, and settling estates. For many common transactions, all that was necessary was being able to copy and use the correct form.

While the requirements weren't particularly difficult, Jackson first needed to improve his elementary skills and basic competency in written English. The school he chose was located a few miles to the north of Waxhaws Creek in a shallow valley. Only a year old, the school was taught by a minister and housed in a primitive log building. It was a humble school with a grand-sounding name: the Bethel Academy. Jackson lived in a boarding house with several other students. He earned his keep as a teacher in a local elementary school, where his job was to keep order in the schoolhouse and teach small children their letters.

After one term he emerged from the Bethel Academy with better grammar and a more refined way of speaking. His genteel manners, though, were never firmly glued to him. When angry, he became animated, lapsed into a marked Irish brogue, and entirely forgot his grammar lessons.

He found a lawyer named Spruce Macay willing to give him a job and the necessary training. Macay lived in Salisbury, North Carolina, a two-hour ride away. In December of 1784—a few months short of his eighteenth birthday—Jackson packed up his possessions, mounted his horse, and rode northward.

Salisbury had a reputation for rollicking taverns and general merriment. The main part of town consisted of two thoroughfares, a few cross streets, and a jumble of mismatched buildings. The courthouse was a small, shabby frame structure. Spruce Macay, one of the wealthiest men in town, owned a thousand acres of land, a dozen horses, and twenty enslaved men and women. His law office, though, was a simple, one-room, wooden structure about fifteen square feet. Jackson spent his days in Macay's office copying papers, running errands, reading law books, studying legal forms, and generally becoming acquainted with the work of a lawyer. When the workday ended, Jackson and his buddies—other young men studying law—went out for wild evenings of card playing, dancing, and whiskey drinking.

By this time, Jackson was well over six feet tall and carried himself ramrod straight—lanky, exuding strength and toughness. He always made a powerful impression on people—and not always in a good way. Lively, talkative, and restless, he was good at competitive games like cards and horse-racing because he had a gut sense of his opponent's weaknesses and felt no remorse in exploiting them. Jackson also had a temper. One day, when a large, burly man tried to pick a fight with him, Jackson responded by snatching a rail from a nearby fence and jamming it into the man's belly so hard he doubled up with pain and fell to the ground, whereupon Jackson stomped on him.

Many of the residents of Salisbury were sure Andrew Jackson would come to no good. Others thought he would get himself killed before long. Years later, when a Salisbury woman learned that Andrew Jackson was running for president, she cried, "What! Jackson up for the President? *Jackson? Andrew* Jackson? The Jackson that used to live in Salisbury? Why, when he was here, he was such a rake that my husband would not bring him into the house! It is true, he might have taken him out to the stable to weight horses for a race, and might drink a glass of whiskey with him there. Well, if Andrew Jackson can be president, anybody can!" In the words of another of Jackson's contemporaries, "Andrew Jackson was the most roaring, rollicking, game-cocking, horse-racing, card-playing, mischievous fellow that ever lived in Salisbury." According to another local resident, Jackson was the "head of all the rowdies hereabouts."

Jackson completed his legal training at the age of twenty, having learned just enough to pass the exam. He appeared before two judges, Samuel Ashe and John F. Williams, for his examination. Both judges found Jackson competent in the law. Once he was authorized to practice, he took odd jobs. For a fee, he would draw up a writ or deed for a client. He supplemented his meager legal fees by gambling and caring for horses. He was arrested once for causing a ruckus. While the details were not recorded, he and a group of buddies were required to pay a large sum in property damage.

His break came about a year later when a friend, John McNairy, was offered a judgeship in Davidson County, located west of the Smokey Mountains in the center of what is now Tennessee but was then the Western District of North Carolina. The most populated settlement, Nashville was nestled on the banks of the Cumberland River. The settlement had been founded only five years earlier.

As a newly appointed judge, McNairy had jobs to offer his friends. Nobody thought anything of the arrangement: A judge needed support, and he rewarded his supporters with jobs. The opportunity was ideal for a young lawyer willing to go west. It was common knowledge that westward beyond the steep mountains lay rich and fertile lands, abundant in natural resources. The rivers abounded with fish. For more than a hundred years, French fur traders had come into the region, drawn by the plentiful wildlife. For many, the wilderness beyond the mountains represented riches waiting to be claimed and possessed.

The problem was that others also claimed the land. Many Americans, including President George Washington and his administration, viewed the Native Americans as sovereign people who owned the land they inhabited. The government therefore entered treaties with the native people over the use of the land. The government's strategy was to promote peace with the Indians by encouraging tribes to adopt Western culture.

Jackson, however, did not believe the Indians owned the land because they didn't *use* it—by which he meant that the Indians didn't build on the land or cultivate it. In Jackson's view, they just roamed over it. Jackson and others who thought the way he did didn't understand why the Indians couldn't just hunt or roam elsewhere. There was plenty of other land for roaming farther west. Not believing the Indians owned the land, many settlers took the land without permission, and if the Indians refused to give up the land peacefully, the settlers mounted attacks. When the Indians fought back and raided white settlements, many settlers viewed the attacks as pure aggression.

Battling with the Indians discouraged many from venturing west, but the prospect of war thrilled Jackson. In fact, he was eager for combat—and eager to seek his fortunes in the West. He wanted the job of prosecuting attorney of the Western District of North Carolina, and he persuaded McNairy to give it to him. A prosecuting attorney, essentially a law enforcement officer, brings lawbreakers to trial. Davidson County was badly in need of a strong prosecuting attorney. The sheriff was weak and incompetent, unable to do anything about one of the problems then facing the settlers: A large number of people had borrowed money from wealthier citizens and were refusing to repay.

The journey would not be easy. Nashville lay two hundred miles to the west. There would be hostile Indians, rivers to ford, and steep and rocky trails. Wolves and bears roamed the woods. When spring came and the snow melted, McNairy, Jackson, and the others who had been awarded jobs formed a small riding party. Jackson armed himself with a rifle and a good set of pistols. He packed a few law books and sheaves of the kind of heavy paper lawyers used. Then he and his riding party headed west.

3

Romance on the Frontier

"With what pleasing hopes I view the future period when I shall be restored to your arms there to spend my days in domestic sweetness with you the dearcompanion of my life never to be separated from you again during this transitory and fluctuating life."

—Andrew Jackson to Rachel Donelson Jackson

In early summer, Jackson's riding party arrived in Jonesborough. They intended to stay just for a few months while the court was in session. Because there were not enough judges—or enough local court business—to keep the courts open all year round, judges rode circuit, visiting a district and holding court for a few months before moving on to the next district.

While in Jonesborough, Jackson applied for permission to practice in the local court. That done, he lined up some legal work to earn extra money. One of his clients, unable to pay in cash, offered an enslaved woman as payment—a young woman named Nancy "about eighteen or twenty years of age." Jackson accepted and thereby acquired his first slave.

Jackson never questioned the morality of slavery. He embraced an attitude known as paternalism, which was widespread at the time. Paternalism holds that there is a natural hierarchy in society with white men at the top and black women at the bottom. Under the doctrine of paternalism, white men are naturally superior. Inferiors—including blacks, women, and Indians—are viewed like children. In the paternalistic worldview, white men, taking on the role of a parent, must care for inferiors, provide for them, and punish them when they misbehave. Corporal punishment at the time was widely accepted, justified by the Biblical verse "Spare the rod, spoil the child." A cornerstone of paternalism was the belief that white women and all people of color were better off under the dominion of white men.

Slavery in America, artist unknown, circa 1830

ABOUT THE TIME Jackson arrived in Jonesborough, the United States Constitution was ratified, replacing the Articles of Confederation. The Articles of Confederation, ratified during the Revolutionary War, had created a loose association of states, in which states retained sovereignty. The Constitution, in setting up a three-part government, created a stronger federal government while weakening the states.

The new Constitution was celebrated in such financial and commercial centers as New York, but many—particularly in the rural areas and along the frontier—viewed the Constitution as the death of liberty.

It didn't take long before the hot-tempered Jackson got into a scrape in Jonesborough. When a lawyer opposing him in the court, Waightstill Avery, used sarcasm to rebut one of Jackson's arguments, he scribbled a note challenging Avery to a duel. The spelling—poor even for Jackson—shows his anger and haste:

> When amans feelings & charector are injured he ought to Seek aspeedy redress; you recd. a few lines from me

Some people in the Carolinas even protested by holding mock funerals, painting coffins black, and burying them. After fighting so long and sacrificing so much during the Revolutionary War, they now faced what they saw as a new threat to their liberty: a government situated far away telling them how to live their lives. Slave owners feared that the federal government would try to outlaw slavery.

While Jackson sympathized with the reason many Southerners objected to the Constitution—namely the fear of giving too much power to the federal government—he came to believe that the nation could be governed under the Constitution while respecting the rights of the states.

yesterday & undoubtedly you understand me. My charector you have Injured; and further you have Insulted me in the presence of a court and a larg audianc I therefore call upon you as a gentleman to give me Satisfaction for the Same; and I further call upon you to give me an answer immediately without Equivocation and I hope you can do without dinner untill the business done; for it is consistant with the charector of agentleman when he Injures aman to make aspedy reparation; therefore I hope you will not fail

in meeting me this day from yr. obt st

Andw. Jackson

P. S. This Evening after court adjourned

Avery declined, having no desire to get himself killed. When the two men left the courthouse, Jackson again demanded the satisfaction of a duel. Reluctantly, Avery agreed. Refusing a duel, according to the standards of the day, was a mark of guilt and the sign of a coward. Andrew and Avery met in a hollow just north of the town. As was customary with duels, witnesses accompanied them. Jackson and Avery paced off the distance between them, and stood facing each other. When one of the witnesses gave the signal, both Avery and Jackson fired at the same time. Fortunately, both missed. Jackson, his honor restored, announced that he had nothing further to settle. He marched forward, shook hands with Avery, and left the dueling grounds.

After the stint in Jonesborough, Jackson, McNairy, and the others in their riding party set out for Nashville. Late one night along the trail, Jackson was awake and vigilant smoking his corncob pipe when he heard Indians signaling to each other by imitating owls. He realized the hooting was not coming from real owls because of the frequency and location of the sounds. Hastily he woke his companions, who confirmed that what Jackson had heard was not owls. The group left the camp and plunged deeper into the forest. Later during the night, a party of hunters came upon their abandoned camp and decided it would be a good place to spend the night, evidently not understanding the meaning of so much concerted hooting of owls. At daybreak, a band of Indians attacked the camp and killed all but one of the hunters.

* * * * * * * * * * * * * * *

Jackson and his party arrived in Nashville on October 26, 1788. From the bluffs, they caught their first sight of the town, which consisted of a courthouse, two stores, two taverns, a distillery, and homes ranging from hastily constructed shacks and log cabins to frame houses with glass windows. The town itself had only a few hundred inhabitants. Most settlers in the area were spread out over various districts. For protection against the Indians, settlers often lived in "stations," or clusters of dwellings surrounded by a fence. One or more of the houses would be fortified against an attack, with heavy wooden shutters and a cellar to provide shelter for the youngest children.

Jackson boarded in the Donelson family station, sharing a

John Overton, date and artist unknown

cabin with another lawyer named John Overton. Rachel Donelson, a widow, was one of Nashville's leading citizens. Within the confines of her station were numerous dwellings inhabited by extended family members and boarders. She was eager to rent a cabin to Jackson and Overton because she wanted more men to help protect the station in the event of an Indian attack.

Another of the cabins in the station was occupied by Mrs. Donelson's twenty-year-old daughter, also named Rachel. The tenth of eleven children and the youngest girl, Rachel was a dark-haired, charming, fun-loving beauty. Friends described her as

Clearing the land for planting. *Plan of an American New Cleared Farm*, artist unknown, 1793.

small with a lovely figure and a pretty oval face "rippling with smiles and dimples." Like Jackson, she had little interest in books and learning, but she loved riding horses and dancing.

Three years earlier, when Rachel was only seventeen, she married a man named Lewis Robards. Rachel's family at the time was living in Kentucky to escape conflicts with the Indians. Not long after Rachel and Robards were married, Rachel's family returned to Nashville. She remained in Kentucky with Robards. Before long, though, she realized she'd made a terrible mistake in marrying Robards, who rapidly became domineering and abusive. He had apparently expected Rachel's personality to change after marriage. When she remained outgoing and lively, he responded with anger and accused her of flirting and encouraging other men. Contemporaries, including Robards's own sister, implied that he physically abused Rachel.

After about two years of marriage, she wrote to her family, telling them of her misery and begging one of her brothers to come get her. Upon receiving the letter, her brother Samuel traveled to Kentucky to bring her home. Robards, determined not to lose her, followed her to Nashville.

This, therefore, was the situation when Jackson arrived: Rachel, high-spirited and beautiful, was the unhappy wife of a jealous man. It was natural for Jackson to find himself attracted to Rachel. It was also natural for Jackson to wish to protect the lovely Rachel from an abusive and overbearing husband. Once, in fact, he stopped Robards near the orchards and accused him of being cruel and unfair to Rachel. Robards instantly suspected Jackson of being in love with his wife, and ordered Jackson to stay away from her. After that, anytime Robards came upon Jackson and Rachel in conversation, he exploded with rage. Given Jackson's own temper, it was a recipe for disaster.

* * * * * * * * * * * * * * *

Meanwhile, Jackson plunged into his legal duties as prosecuting attorney. He and John Overton operated their law offices from their home. Before long, Jackson had forced seventy debtors to pay their outstanding balances. His tactics were unorthodox, to say the least, and often included threats of violence. One day, one of the debtors, furious at Jackson, showed his irritation by deliberately stepping on Jackson's foot. Jackson responded by picking up a piece of wood and knocking the man out cold. In the words of one historian, respect for the law, Jackson style, had arrived in Nashville.

It wasn't long before Jackson was called to help fight a band of Indians who had attacked a station in the vicinity. Jackson and about twenty other men pursued them to their camp on the south side of the Duck River. Through the night, Jackson and his team hid in the thick cane. In the morning, they attacked. The team killed a few of the Indians. The others escaped across the river. The team then returned and raided the Indian camp, capturing sixteen guns, nineteen shot pouches, blankets, leggings, and moccasins. Jackson startled his companions with his sheer enjoyment of the escapade.

Cherokees attack a Tennessee station. From Amos Kendall, *Life of General Jackson,* 1843.

By the summer of 1789, town gossips were reporting that Jackson and Rachel were in love. When the rumors reached Robards, he was furious and accused Rachel of becoming intimate with Jackson. What galled Robards was that Rachel's family was turning away from him and favoring Jackson—who was unfailingly polite to Rachel and her mother, and indeed, all the women in the station.

Rachel protested her innocence, insisting that she and Jackson were merely friends. Jackson responded to Robards's accusation by threatening to cut off Robards's ears if he didn't stop slandering Rachel. When Robards didn't stop accusing Rachel of being unfaithful, Jackson offered to settle their quarrel with a duel.

Robards refused the challenge. Instead, he went to the magistrate, a local official appointed by McNairy, and swore out a warrant for Jackson's arrest. Guards from the Donelson's blockhouse escorted Jackson to court. As the parties were on their way to the courthouse, Jackson asked to borrow one of the guard's knives. At first the guard refused. Jackson promised he intended to do no harm, so the guard handed him the knife. When they arrived, Robards was waiting. Jackson touched the knife point and looked menacingly at Robards, who, frightened, ran from the

Rachel Donelson, painted by Howard Chandler Christy, 1941, from contemporary paintings by Ralph E. W. Earl, circa 1825. Because no paintings exist of Rachel as a young woman, the artist imagined her as a young woman from paintings of when she was older.

courthouse. The magistrate promptly dismissed the complaint against Jackson on the grounds that the complaining party had left the courthouse.

Sometime within the year—the chronology isn't clear—Jackson and Rachel ran off together to Natchez, a leading town on the Mississippi River, located in what is now the state of Mississippi, but was then under control of the Spanish. Legal divorce at the time was almost impossible to obtain—and was rarely granted to a woman. Unhappy couples in the backcountry and along the frontier often dissolved their own marriages. The American Revolution convinced many that self-divorce was perfectly acceptable: If colonists could overthrow an oppressive government, why shouldn't an unhappy couple overthrow oppressive marriage vows? Visitors to the backcountry condemned the practice as both illegal and uncivilized, but the practice of couples declaring themselves divorced, then remarrying without formalities, was commonplace in the western borderlands of the South.

After Rachel and Jackson ran away to Natchez, Robards went back to Kentucky. Rachel and Jackson remained for a short time in Natchez, where they lived as man and wife. When they returned to Nashville, Rachel's family and the Nashville community accepted them as a properly married couple.

Jackson had bought a small plantation where the Cumberland River made a U-shaped bend. With money earned from his law practice, he bought more land and added to his number of enslaved men and women. He often accepted land or slaves in exchange for legal fees, so his landholdings and number of enslaved workers grew.

Jackson enjoyed being a member of the tightly knit Donelson clan. Family connections were important in the South, so being a Donelson heightened his status. Under the Southern honor code, family members defended one another's honor. Thus a person without family was at a distinct disadvantage. About a year after Jackson became a member of the Donelson family, on October 8, 1791, he was elected a trustee of the Davidson Academy, a group of citizen leaders of the community. Jackson, being ambitious, boldly wrote letters to the most important men in Tennessee, introducing himself and offering advice and assistance.

Meanwhile, Robards sued for divorce in Kentucky. A Kentucky jury found Rachel guilty of desertion and adultery and granted the divorce. When—or if—Jackson and Rachel exchanged wedding vows, or whether they were content to live as common-law man and wife is unknown.

Jackson and Rachel lived together happily. Rachel's gentleness and soft, lilting voice calmed Jackson. She disliked swearing, so he was always careful with his language around her. Instead of his usual vulgarities, when she was near he would express anger by saying, "by Jupiter!" or "by the eternal!" She, too, changed after marriage. Her wildness and vivacity gave way to a deep piousness and a passion for domestic life. Everyone who knew them agreed they were a perfect match and very much in love.

4

Congressman Jackson

"[M]ischief springs from the power which the moneyed interest derives from a paper currency which they are able to control, from the multitude of corporations with exclusive privileges which they have succeeded in obtaining in the different States, and which are employed altogether for their benefit."

—Andrew Jackson

As a way of acquiring additional wealth, Jackson became a land speculator. Land speculating, popular in early America, involved buying large tracts of land the moment they became available to the public, holding on to them until prices rose, then selling at a large profit. In March of 1795, Jackson traveled to Philadelphia—his first time in a Northern state—to sell 50,000 acres of land he held jointly with his partner, John Overton. He found a buyer, an old friend named David Allison. When

Jackson accepted his offer, Allison paid with promissory notes.

Jackson and Overton intended to use the money from the sale of their land to open a trading post on the Cumberland River. To get the trading post started, Jackson used one of the promissory notes to purchase goods from a Philadelphia company called Meeker, Cochran, and Company. He endorsed the note to the company by signing his name. The company accepted the endorsed note and treated it like cash. Jackson used the other notes to make other purchases.

Two months later, Jackson received a shock: Allison declared bankruptcy, rendering his promissory notes worthless.

Philadelphia as it appeared when Jackson first visited. South East Corner of Third and Market Streets. Engraving by Wm. Birch & Sons, 1800.

THE FEDERAL GOVERNMENT at the time issued a small amount of currency in the form of gold and silver coins, called specie or hard money. Americans bought and sold property or goods using banknotes issued by chartered banks. Under the economic system known as the gold standard—the standard used in the United States until 1933—a bank was supposed to hold gold coins in its vaults to cover any notes issued so that anyone holding a bank note could exchange the note for gold at any time. Promissory notes—like checks, bills of exchange, cashier's checks, and banknotes—are *negotiable instruments*, or legal documents that guarantee a specific payment of hard money.

Today, no country uses a gold standard. Most economists now agree that the supply of gold fluctuates too much, and nations would too easily be able to play havoc with each other's economy by demanding gold for bills and thus depleting the country's gold supply.

When the notes came due, Meeker, Cochran, and Company demanded payment. Jackson was stunned to learn that he was required to cover the payment and thus had to come up with the cash himself. He and Overton sank deeply into debt.

Jackson was furious. He claimed that he didn't understand that in endorsing the notes and using them as cash, he was accepting full legal responsibility for their payment—an astonishing admission of ignorance from someone trained in the law. As a result, he developed a passionate hatred of paper money, debt, promissory notes, and banks. He viewed bankers as pure evil, out to swindle ordinary Americans who didn't understand the complicated rules of finance. He never again trusted anything as abstract as bank notes or paper money. He trusted only land he could see and gold that he could put between his teeth and bite.

★ ★ ★ ★ ★ ★ ★ ★ ★ ★ ★ ★ ★ ★ ★

As Nashville and other Tennessee settlements grew, tensions and skirmishes between the Indians and settlers escalated. The federal government believed the solution was simple: White settlers must stop stealing Indian lands. President George Washington and his secretary of war, John Knox, persuaded Congress to pass the Trade and Intercourse Act of 1790, a law that imposed penalties on whites who entered tribal lands without a permit. Knox argued that any other approach "would be a gross violation of the fundamental laws of nature and of that distributive justice which is the glory of a nation."

Jackson railed against the federal law. His view was that Indians were like children who tended to be cruel and vicious and needed stern punishment to force them to behave in a civilized manner. You don't *reason* with Indians, Jackson believed. You *tell* them. "What motives Congress are governed by with Respect to their pacific Disposition towards Indians I know not," he wrote. "Some say humanity dictates it; but certainly she ought to extend an equal share of humanity to her own citizens; in doing this, Congress should act justly and punish the barbarians for murdering her innocent citizens."

Jackson, and others on the Tennessee frontier, openly defied the federal laws by attacking Indian villages whenever they believed doing so would keep their own settlements safe. During one of Jackson's raids against the Indians, he and a fellow resident of Nashville were reconnoitering around Knoxville when they rode directly into an Indian ambush. Jackson escaped, but his companion was killed.

In 1796, partly as a way to deal with what it considered the Indian problem, Tennessee applied for statehood.

THE UNITED STATES CONSTITUTION says very little about Native Americans. Article 1, Section 2 excludes Indians not taxed from the census. Article 1, Section 8, gives Congress power to regulate "commerce with foreign nations, and among the states, and with the Indian Tribes"—a clause commonly referred to as the Commerce Clause.

At the same time, Article IV, Section 3 states that "no new State shall be formed or erected within the Jurisdiction of any other state." The Tennessee government believed that allowing Indians sovereignty within state borders was tantamount to forming a new state within a state, which violated Article IV, section 3. Dismissing the Commerce Clause as not applying to matters within state boundaries, Tennessee officials believed that once they became a state, Indians within its borders would not enjoy sovereignty or protection from federal treaties.

Congressman Jackson

After Tennessee was admitted to the Union as the sixteenth state, Jackson participated in writing the state constitution. Afterward, officials of the newly formed state government asked Jackson to run for Tennessee's seat in the United States House of Representatives. Jackson agreed, so in the fall of 1796, he ran unopposed, and was elected Tennessee's first congressman. In Tennessee during this period, as in most other states, the legislature selected the state's congressmen and senators.

For the second time, Jackson set off for Philadelphia. He arrived in December of 1797, as George Washington was finishing his second term of office. Not long after Jackson settled into his duties as congressman from Tennessee, the United States House of Representatives drafted a resolution thanking George Washington for his services to the country. When the resolution came up for a vote, Jackson voted *nay*, joining eleven other representatives from Western regions who also resented Washington's policies toward the Native people.

When the federal government sought to chastise settlers in Tennessee for raids upon Native Americans, Jackson took the floor. Demonstrating his natural flair for speechmaking—and making clear his views that the Indians were the aggressors and the settlers entirely innocent—he said, "When it was seen that war was waged upon the state, that the knife and the tomahawk were held over the heads of women and children, that peaceable citizens were murdered, it was time to make resistance." He convinced enough of his fellow congressmen that the citizens of Tennessee had no choice but to defend themselves that he succeeded in persuading Congress not to chastise the settlers, but instead to compensate them for their expenses in carrying out the raids.

Jackson and his allies were known as political conservatives—they advocated states' rights and a limited federal government. In keeping with his political conservatism, Jackson voted against a direct tax and a provision that would raise the salaries of federal government employees. His *nay* vote against George Washington, his vote against a salary raise for government employees, and the fact that he'd secured federal money to compensate Tennessee in its Indian wars made him something of a folk hero in Tennessee and along the frontier.

He disliked living in Philadelphia, though. He was homesick, and felt surrounded by values and attitudes he considered elitist. He was aware that the wealthy, well-educated, and well-heeled Easterners looked down on his bad grammar, his country way of talking, and his lack of a classical education, and it pricked his pride.

Alexander Hamilton was no longer secretary of the Treasury—he had resigned two years earlier—but his influence and legacy was everywhere, in the bustling commerce and imposing First Bank of the United States, with its complicated system of securities and interest. The economy of early America had been mostly agrarian, meaning that most families were farmers who grew or made almost everything they needed at home. By the time Jackson arrived in Philadelphia, America was rapidly changing from an agrarian nation into an industrial one. Power looms, invented in the 1780s, made possible mass production of clothing, and steamboats, which came into use during the 1790s, allowed for travel in both directions on a river. Ease of travel allowed Americans in remote areas access to newspapers, thus enabling them to remain informed of national events and make their voices heard.

Like Thomas Jefferson, who would soon serve as vice president under the newly elected John Adams, Andrew Jackson believed that the booms in industry and banking were corrupting America. Corruption in the late eighteenth and early nineteenth centuries did not simply mean dishonesty for personal gain, or illegal activity like theft or embezzlement (people in power abusing their position of trust to steal). Corruption also meant to degrade the quality of something, or to lower the moral standards of the society.

Jackson believed that banking and industry—by consolidating money and power into the hands of a few—were re-creating a British-style aristocracy, exactly what his brothers and mother had given their lives to drive from American shores. In his view, bankers didn't labor or create anything. All they did was manipulate numbers. He didn't see plantation owners with hundreds of slaves toiling in the field as aristocrats. The plantation owner, in his view, was a simple planter, earning an honest living from the land. Even after Jackson had 150 slaves working his fields for him, he always referred to his plantation as his farm. He saw no irony in calling himself a simple farmer while enslaved men and women performed the labor.

* * * * * * * * * * * * * * *

Jackson returned to Tennessee after a single term, declaring himself finished with Philadelphia and Congress. He was glad to be back. The Jacksons' home was always bustling, and Jackson enjoyed family life. After several years of marriage, he and Rachel still had no children of their own, so they filled their house with other people's children and even became guardians to orphans and children whose parents were unable to raise them. Because Rachel had ten siblings, flocks of nieces and nephews stayed with them for long visits. Their home was joyful, but their marriage remained childless, a source of sadness for both of them.

Not long after Jackson returned to Tennessee, one of Tennessee's Senators, William Blount, was expelled from the Senate for crooked land dealings. The Tennessee legislature appointed Jackson to finish out his term. Reluctantly, Jackson agreed to return to Philadelphia, but at the end of seven months in the nation's capital, when the term was finished, he was ready to go home, and stay home.

The job he had his eye on was justice of the Tennessee Superior Court—a position that would suit him better than senator or congressman. While requiring him to travel around Tennessee, the job would nonetheless keep him closer to home. The position of judge would allow him to become acquainted with the most important men in Tennessee, an appealing idea to a man as ambitious as Jackson. The position of judge was particularly attractive because it carried a salary of $600 per year in gold, only $200 less than the salary given to the governor, the highest paid position in the state.

Jackson was thirty-one when he ran unopposed and became a judge, thus opening a new chapter in his life.

5

Justice, Jackson Style

"I am of the opinion that a good judiciary lends much to the dignity of a state and the happiness of the people."

—Andrew Jackson

Jackson enjoyed being a judge. Backwoods courthouses were often crude structures with sawdust and spit on the floors, but Jackson insisted on decorum and respect. He took a blunt, commonsense approach to judging and to the law. In the words of one of his contemporaries, his decisions were "short, untechnical, unlearned, sometimes ungrammatical, and generally right." At the end of trials, he often told juries, "Do what is right between the parties. That is what the law always means."

There was never a backlog in Jackson's court. He dispensed justice with stunning swiftness. Because he didn't worry about technical points or what a more educated jurist might consider the nuances of the law, he could resolve as many as three or four cases in a single day. His popularity and circle of admirers grew.

His handling of the case of Russell Bean—a large, lumbering, burly man—became legendary. Russell Bean claimed that his wife was unfaithful to him and had given birth to another man's baby. As a result, he quarreled with his wife and, in a drunken rage, cut off the infant's ear. He justified the brutality by saying he wanted to teach his wife a lesson.

The sheriff hauled Russell Bean into the courthouse. Bean stomped around, cursing at everyone, and then stormed out. Jackson ordered the sheriff to bring him back. The sheriff tried, but returned and explained that he couldn't do it. Bean was waving his pistols, threatening to shoot anyone who came within ten feet of him. Nobody dared approach.

Judge Jackson called a ten-minute recess. He picked up his own pistols and marched from the courthouse. He found Russell Bean in the street, in the middle of a crowd, cursing and waving a pistol in each hand. Jackson marched up to Bean, stared right

Russell Bean surrendering to Judge Jackson. From Amos Kendall, *Life of General Jackson*, 1843.

into his eyes, and said, "Now, surrender, you infernal villain, this very instant, or I'll blow you through!"

Bean lowered his pistols. "There, there, judge," he said. "It's no use. I give in."

Later, Bean explained why he had given up so easily: "Why when he came up, I looked him in the eye, and I saw shoot, and there wasn't shoot in nary other eye in the crowd; and so I says to myself, says I, hoss, it's about time to sing small, and so I did."

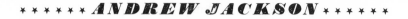

Jackson hungered for glory on the battlefield. With an eye to running for major general, he cultivated the friendship of military officers throughout the state. He learned the art of playing politics—offering favors in return for favors.

Portrait of Andrew Jackson, Ralph E. W. Earl, 1815

After six years as a judge, Jackson announced his candidacy for major general of the Tennessee militia, the highest ranking military officer in the state. His opposition in the election was John Sevier, a popular Revolutionary War hero. Sevier was shocked that Jackson—a lawyer without any military experience—dared challenge him. The election was bitter, with both candidates hurling accusations at the other. When the votes were counted, seventeen members of the legislature voted for Jackson, and seventeen for Sevier. It was up to the governor to break the tie.

The governor, Archibald Roane, was a friend of Jackson's. In addition to Roane's personal friendship, Jackson had what he considered an ace up his sleeve. In his possession was damning evidence that Sevier had engaged in land fraud. His evidence included an affidavit from an official of Washington County and supporting documents. The evidence stood to benefit Roane as well as Jackson because Roane knew Sevier would soon challenge him for the governorship. As Roane was deliberating on which man to choose, Jackson privately showed Roane his evidence against Sevier. Roane appointed Jackson major general of Tennessee. He still retained his position as judge.

The following year, when Sevier challenged Roane for the governorship, Roane made public the evidence Jackson had showed him. Jackson had to substantiate the charges—which he did. Sevier, outraged, swore that the evidence was false and politically motivated. He vowed revenge against Jackson.

Jackson and Sevier met in person in Knoxville in October of 1803. Jackson, finishing out his term as judge, arrived in Knoxville to hold court. While walking through a public square, he found himself face-to-face with Sevier. For a moment the two men faced each other in stunned silence. Then Sevier went on the attack, accusing Jackson of pretensions, of being nothing more than a pitiful lawyer who dared aspire to military office. Jackson, caught off guard by the insults, defended himself by citing his services to the state and the country.

"Services?" Sevier laughed. "I know of no great service you have rendered the country, except taking a trip to Natchez with another man's wife."

"Great God!" Jackson yelled, enraged. "Do you mention *her* sacred name?"

Both Jackson and Sevier drew their pistols. Men leaped forward to separate them, but one of them fired. The bullet grazed a bystander. The incident ended with nobody seriously harmed. Both men, still furious, went their separate ways. Jackson, though, would not let such an insult go unanswered. As soon as he could get his hands on paper and pen, he scribbled a challenge to a duel. Sevier refused. Jackson issued another challenge, and again Sevier refused. So Jackson went in search of him. He found him riding with several men, including two of his grown sons. Jackson drew his pistol, dismounted, and drew a second pistol. Sevier leaped from his horse and drew both his pistols.

The two men, clutching their pistols, hurled insults at each other. Then Sevier ducked behind a tree to get out of Jackson's line of fire. One of Sevier's sons aimed at Jackson. Jackson responded by aiming at Sevier's other son. The tension was relieved when a member of Sevier's party rushed forward, making friendly gestures.

The story spread throughout the state. As always, whatever Jackson said or did quickly became fashionable. The curse he had uttered, "Great God!" became a favorite in Tennessee.

* * * * * * * * * * * * * * *

As major general, Jackson supervised drills and learned to manage military units while waiting to be called to the battlefield. Meanwhile, still struggling to pay off the debt from the Allison land-speculating fiasco, he sold his plantation and an additional twenty-five thousand acres. He then bought a more modest plantation, 420 acres of fields and woods, ten miles from Nashville. On the property was a simple block house with a large downstairs room and two bedrooms upstairs. Jackson and Rachel named their new plantation the Hermitage.

The Jacksons entertained often, so their home was boisterous and lively. Anyone of importance who came to Tennessee could expect an invitation to the home of Andrew Jackson, major general of Tennessee. By this time, Jackson had a fearsome reputation, so first-time visitors often expected to be greeted by a pistol-toting madman with blazing eyes. Instead, they were startled to discover a man who exuded charm and warmth—as well as raw vitality and energy. According to one visitor, Jackson "affected no style, and put on no airs of greatness."

A drawing of the Jacksons' first home on the Hermitage property. Courtesy of the Andrew Jackson Foundation, Nashville, Tennessee.

Other than the Bible, which Jackson and Rachel read regularly, neither had any interest in books. Jackson, however, was a devoted reader of newspapers, subscribing to no fewer than twenty. He kept up with the news, not only from his newspapers, but from visitors. As a result, he was a good conversationalist, listening attentively and responding with wit and grace.

Under Rachel's careful management, the plantation became increasingly profitable, producing quantities of cotton, corn, and wheat. Jackson believed he treated his enslaved men and women decently because, in his view, they were well fed and clothed, and worked in moderation. He also remarked that he knew that "negroes will complain without cause."

Jackson expected his enslaved workers to accept complete subjugation, and he did not hesitate to whip slaves who dared to question their inferior status. He threatened the public lashing of one enslaved woman after Rachel told him that she was putting on airs and behaving with impudence. If a slave ran away, he showed no mercy. After one slave ran away, he placed an advertisement offering a reward for anyone who would capture and return the slave. He also promised to pay an extra ten dollars for every one hundred lashes given to the slave.

In May of 1805, a distinguished—and notorious—man arrived in Tennessee: Aaron Burr, former vice president of the United States and the man who, the year before, had killed Alexander Hamilton in a duel. Burr, now a social outcast in the East, where he was viewed as an assassin and villain, headed west, to where he was held in higher esteem. Duels along the frontier were legal and earned men respect. Moreover, throughout the South and along the frontier, Hamilton was despised as a man who loved bankers and industrialists, who had helped to build a strong federal government, and who had worked firmly against the interests of Southern slaveholders. Aaron Burr was popular in Tennessee, not only for killing Alexander Hamilton, but because he had helped Tennessee obtain statehood.

Nashville welcomed Burr with a cannon salute, the waving of flags, and dinners in his honor. People came from miles around to see him. He spent five days as the Jacksons' guest at the Hermitage, where he talked about a plan to fight the Spanish in order to seize more territory for the United States. He claimed that Henry Dearborn, the secretary of war under President Jefferson, knew of his plans and approved. Jackson was charmed and impressed by the cultivated and elegant Burr.

Jackson, eager for military action, embraced the idea of

expelling the Spanish from North America and acquiring more territory for the United States. He worried about the Spanish along the southwestern border. He didn't believe the United States would be safe until the Spanish were subdued and the borders were secure. Moreover, war with Spain, in his view, would be "a handsome theatre for our enterprising young men and a source of acquiring fame." When Burr went to Kentucky to gather an army, Jackson helped secure boats and other provisions for a raid on Spanish territories.

In November, Jackson suspected from chance remarks dropped by a mutual acquaintance that Burr had duped him and that the plot was actually treason against the United States. He suspected that Burr's true intention was to seize New Orleans, conquer Mexico, and annex the Western part of the United States into a new empire, headed by Burr and a friend of his, a Southern general then serving in New Orleans. Jackson's fears were borne out when Burr was arrested in Kentucky and accused of raising troops for illegal purposes. The charges against Burr were dismissed for lack of evidence, but Jackson remained wary.

Burr returned to Tennessee and assured Jackson that he had no intention of committing treason against the United States. Once again, Jackson believed him. Then in late December,

Jefferson issued a proclamation declaring that military treason was in progress against the United States. Nashville panicked. On January 1, 1807, Jackson received orders from Jefferson and Secretary of War Henry Dearborn to prepare his command to protect the United States.

Jackson summoned his troops and made such a show of strength that the people of Nashville felt reassured. The panic subsided. Burr was captured in the wilderness of Mississippi and brought to Virginia for trial. Eventually Burr was found not guilty because once again there wasn't enough evidence against him, but for a long time, Jackson's association with Burr tainted him among those in the East.

★ ★ ★ ★ ★ ★ ★ ★ ★ ★ ★ ★ ★ ★ ★

Jackson and a man named Charles Dickinson were rival horse breeders. A feud between them broke out when Dickinson accused Jackson of reneging on a promise. Then Dickinson committed the unpardonable sin of accusing Rachel of being married to two men at once. Enraged that Dickinson had taken Rachel's "sacred" name into his "polluted mouth," Jackson placed a notice in a local newspaper demanding satisfaction and calling Dickinson a "blackguard." Dickinson responded by placing his own notice calling Jackson a "worthless scoundrel."

Dickinson and Jackson agreed to meet on the dueling grounds at the break of dawn. Dickinson was reportedly the best shot in Tennessee. He also had a reputation as a snapshot—he fired quickly and was usually accurate. Jackson's strategy was to stand by and let Dickinson shoot first in the hopes that the shot would not be deadly, giving him time to aim carefully.

The duelists raised their pistols. Dickinson fired first. Dust rose from Jackson's coat, but Jackson remained standing. "Great God!" Dickinson cried. "Have I missed him?" In fact, a bullet had lodged in Jackson's chest. Ignoring the searing pain, Jackson raised his pistol and took aim. Later he said he would have summoned the strength to shoot Dickinson even if Dickinson had shot him through the brain. Jackson squeezed the trigger. There was only a click. The hammer stopped at half cock. Jackson drew back the hammer again, took aim, and fired. The bullet entered just below Dickinson's ribs, killing him.

When the word went out of what had happened, people were scandalized. According to the etiquette of duels, once Jackson's gun failed to fire, the duel was over. Taking careful aim and squeezing the trigger a second time amounted to killing a defenseless man in cold blood. For several months, Jackson was a social outcast. His defenders pointed out that Jackson fired a second time because he fully believed his own wound was fatal and he didn't want to die without exacting revenge. The duel, combined with his quarrel with Sevier, firmly established his reputation for being violent and vengeful.

Dickinson's bullet had lodged in Jackson's chest too close to his heart for a surgeon to dare try to remove it. He thus carried Dickinson's bullet in his chest for the rest of his life.

On December 22, 1809, twin boys were born to Rachel's brother and his wife, Severn. The mother was too weak to care for two children, so she allowed Jackson and Rachel to adopt one of the boys. Jackson and Rachel, thrilled to be parents at last, named their new son Andrew Jackson, Jr.

Andrew Jackson Jr., Jackson's adopted son at the age of eleven. Ralph E. W. Earl, 1820.

6

The Beat of the War Drum

"The hour of national vengeance is now at hand. The eternal enemies of American prosperity are again to be taught to respect your rights, after having been compelled to feel, once more, the power of your arms."

—Andrew Jackson

Jackson pored over his newspapers, thrilled by reports that the United States and Britain were moving toward war. The British were seizing American ships, accusing the American seamen aboard of being British deserters, taking them as captives, and forcing them to work on British ships. Because so many Americans had recently immigrated from Great Britain or were the children of British immigrants, American sailors often looked and talked exactly like their British counterparts. The British imprisoned them on the grounds that they were rebellious subjects of the Crown. Between 1803 and 1812, the British captured about six thousand American seamen.

The underlying message for Jackson and others was that the British still didn't recognize American independence. Other Europeans as well often looked at Americans as nothing more than rebellious and unruly. Many refused to take America seriously as an independent nation on the grounds that the colonists had won the Revolutionary War only because the colonies had received help from France.

For Jackson, the British insults were personal. The British, after all, were the enemies of his ancestors. He carried a scar on his head from the blow of a British officer. His mother and brothers had died in the Revolution. Jackson, eager for war with Britain, believed it was time for the United States to flex its muscles and establish American sovereignty once and for all.

President Jefferson, however, wanted to avoid war. In the hopes of subduing the British, Jefferson imposed a trade embargo on Britain—but the embargo harmed American businesses as much as the British and was unpopular among voters. When James Madison succeeded Jefferson as president in 1809, he, too, resisted leading the country into war, believing America was too poorly equipped for all-out warfare.

James Madison, fourth president of the United States. Painting by John Vanderlyn, 1915.

Jackson scoffed at what he called the fearful old grannies in Washington and elsewhere who wanted to avoid war. These included the merchants and bankers who were afraid war would hurt their economic interests and Quakers and others who believed war was morally wrong.

President James Madison felt growing pressure from a group of young congressmen who Jefferson called the War Hawks. The War Hawks clamored for war in a desire to drive all Europeans from North America, thereby securing the borders. This meant taking possession of both Canada and Florida. Jackson agreed with the War Hawks. For Jackson, though, it wasn't enough to expel all Europeans from North America. To secure the borders, he believed the Indian tribes needed to be brought under American control, too.

With the coming of war, Tecumseh, a Shawnee war chief

Chief Tecumseh. This drawing first appeared in Benson Lossing's book *Pictorial Field Book of the War of 1812*, published in 1868.

from Ohio, saw the opportunity to stop American westward expansion and protect Indian ancestral lands. He sought to unite the tribes and build a confederation of Indian nations in alliance with the British. More than a dozen Indian nations joined his coalition. In Jackson's view, the British were stirring the Indians to attack Americans. The Indian view was that they were preparing to fight a great war for tribal independence.

In February of 1812, Congress authorized the enlistment of fifty thousand soldiers. Then, on June 18, 1812, Congress declared war on Great Britain. President James Madison signed the declaration.

Jackson, thrilled, sent out a stirring call for enlistees in Tennessee. "*Citizens!* Your government has at last yielded to the impulse of the nation," he wrote. "*Who are we? And for what are we going to fight?* are we the titled slaves of George the third?

The military conscripts of Napolon [sic] the great? Or the frozen peasants of the Russian Czar? No—we are the free born sons of America, the citizens of the only republic now existing in the world, and the only people on earth who possess rights, liberties and property which they dare call their own." He soon had two thousand volunteers.

Jackson eagerly awaited the call to lead his men into battle. When his entreaties to join the fighting were ignored, he believed he was being punished for his association with Aaron Burr. Sitting on the sidelines was particularly frustrating because the British were giving the Americans a beating. General Henry Dearborn attempted to conquer Canada, and failed. General William Hull surrendered Detroit to an army of British and Indian soldiers without firing a shot. Jackson seethed, swearing that if he had been in command of either of those missions, the outcome would have been different.

At last, in January of 1813, the secretary of war issued orders for Jackson to lead his army south to defend New Orleans, an important gateway and the nation's second-busiest port after New York.

That winter was particularly harsh. The day Jackson's army marched from Tennessee, a foot of snow lay on the ground.

After the first night, all the firewood the army carried had been burned for warmth. Each day they had to scramble for food and wood.

Thirty-nine days and five hundred miles later, Jackson and his men arrived in Natchez only to receive word from John Armstrong, secretary of war, that the mission was aborted. "Sir," wrote Armstrong, "the causes embodying and marching to New Orleans the Corps under our command having ceased to exist, you will on receipt of this letter, consider it as dismissed from public service . . ."

Jackson was stunned—and furious. Here he was, five hundred miles from home, without adequate food or medicine or shelter, and he was expected to dissolve his army in the heart of Indian country? The orders, to Jackson, were nothing short of lunacy, so he disobeyed them. Instead of disbanding, he marched with his men all the way back to Tennessee. His next letter to Rachel ended with, "Kiss my little Andrew for me and tell him his papa is coming home."

Jackson and his men marched back through frozen woods. Many fell ill. Jackson himself walked so that a sick soldier could have his horse. He saw it as his duty to "act as a father to the sick and to the well" and stay with them until they entered Nashville.

He led his men with such grit and fortitude that he earned the nickname that stuck for the rest of his life: Old Hickory.

* * * * * * * * * * * * * * *

Soon after Jackson returned to Tennessee, he was asked to supervise a duel between two men, Billy Carroll and Jesse Benton. The duel took place on June 14, 1813. After the signal was given to shoot, Benton squatted down to make the smallest possible target. Carroll's bullet grazed his buttocks. Shot in the rear! Benton became the laughingstock of Tennessee. Thomas Benton, Jesse's brother, accused Jackson of conducting a savage, unequal, and unfair duel, claiming that his brother didn't understand the complicated rules. Jackson never let an insult or a challenge go unanswered. The next time Jackson and the Benton brothers came face-to-face was in front of a Nashville hotel. Thomas Benton growled that he planned to punish Jackson, so Jackson should defend himself. Jackson drew his gun and backed Thomas into the hotel. Jesse ducked into the barroom and from the doorway, raised his pistol and fired at Jackson, hitting him in the arm and shoulder. Jackson pitched forward and fired at Jesse as he fell. He missed. Thomas fired twice before bystanders rushed forward to stop the fighting.

Friends carried Jackson to a hotel room and called a doctor. Before slipping into unconsciousness, Jackson forbade the doctor to amputate his arm. Jackson recovered, and carried the bullet in his arm for twenty years, until at last he allowed a doctor to remove it.

✶ ✶ ✶ ✶ ✶ ✶ ✶ ✶ ✶ ✶ ✶ ✶ ✶ ✶ ✶

The Muskogee Nation, called the Creeks by white settlers because of their skill in traversing waterways, was divided on whether to join Chief Tecumseh's alliance of tribes. Some wanted to fight the Americans to prevent westward expansion; others feared that war with the United States would leave them worse off. The leader of the faction that wanted to fight, Red Eagle, was mixed race and had two names: Red Eagle, from his mother, and William Weatherford, from his Scottish grandfather. Red Eagle was opposed to the killing of civilians, but he agreed to lead a band of warriors against Fort Mims in what is now Alabama. Never before had Indian warriors succeeded in storming a fort, so Red Eagle expected his men to make a token attack and then retreat to avoid loss of lives.

His band of warriors arrived at Fort Mims on a hot and humid day in August and was shocked to find the gates of the fort open and the inhabitants lazing in the shade. Red Eagle could not hold his warriors back. They rushed the entrance. What followed was a massacre. Of the 553 people inside, including numerous civilians, women, and children, only forty lives were spared.

News of the attack sent waves of fury and panic along the frontier. Citizens of Nashville demanded a war to exterminate the Muskogee Nation. Jackson, recovering from his gunshot wounds, wrote a letter from his bed declaring, "The health of your general is restored. He will command in person." The letter he wrote calling for volunteers showed his attitude toward the Native people, and his ability to arouse anger and fear through stirring rhetoric:

> Brave Tennesseans!
>
> Your frontier is threatened with invasion by the savage foe! Already do they advance towards your frontier with their scalping knifes unsheathed, to butcher your wives, your children, and your helpless babes. Time is not to be lost. We must hasten to the frontier, or we will find it drenched in the blood of our fellow-citizens.

Among the twenty-five hundred citizens who volunteered to fight the Muskogee under the command of Andrew Jackson was Sam Houston, later known for his role in bringing Texas into the Union, and Davy Crockett, who would become a legendary frontiersman.

Jackson, his arm and shoulder bandaged tightly enough to stop the flow of blood, devised a simple and brutal strategy. He planned to march into Muskogee territory, "laying waste their villages, burning their houses, killing their warriors, and leading into captivity their wives and children."

On October 7, 1813, his arm in a sling, Jackson took command of his army. Just under a month later, they reached the Muskogee village of Tallushatchee. One thousand of Jackson's troops encircled the village, slaughtered every man, and marched the women and children away as captives. Later Davy Crockett reported that Jackson and his soldiers burned houses with the inhabitants inside, and when Indians tried to flee, they "shot them like dogs."

In a move that many saw as contradicting his reputation as a violent and vengeful killer but perfectly in keeping with his paternalistic views toward Indians, Jackson rescued an orphaned infant from the battlefield. Jackson brought the child to his tent, dissolved some brown sugar in water and coaxed him to drink. He named the baby Lyncoya and sent him to the Hermitage as a playmate for Andrew Jr., with a note to Rachel that said, "when I reflect that he as to his relations is so much like myself I feel an unusual sympathy for him." He also commented that the child "is a savage, but one that fortune has thrown on my hands." Lyncoya lived at the Hermitage until he died of tuberculosis at the age of sixteen.

Jackson attacked one Indian village after another in a campaign of fire and killing. As the months wore on, Jackson's army grew weary and hungry. They'd run out of supplies and often had nothing to eat except acorns. Jackson did his best to secure supplies, but had little success. Tempers flared. A group of volunteers announced that they'd had enough. They had enlisted to fight Indians, not starve. Jackson, enraged by the idea that any of his soldiers would even *consider* desertion, grabbed a musket, rode into the path of the group of deserters, and growled that he'd shoot the first man who took another step. Nobody moved.

Then came the incident with eighteen-year-old John Woods, who had been standing guard one cold rainy night. After receiving permission from an officer to leave his post, Woods returned to his tent for a blanket. He sat down to eat breakfast. When another officer ordered him back to his post, he refused. The officer ordered Woods arrested, and Woods went berserk—grabbing his gun and swearing he would shoot the first person who laid a hand on him. Someone cried "Mutiny" and Jackson sprang to action. Determined to set an example, he had Woods court-martialed. After a brief trial, he ordered Woods executed.

The execution of John Woods put an end to any talk of desertion, but Jackson could not prevent the majority of his

Jackson threatens to shoot anyone who tries to desert. From Amos Kendall, *Life of General Jackson*, 1843.

army from returning home as soon as their one-year period of enlistment ended—leaving him alone with a war to fight but no soldiers. The arrival of eight hundred new volunteers in January of 1814 followed by twenty-five hundred in March allowed him to continue.

With a total force of about four thousand men, Jackson's army overwhelmed the Muskogee warriors at Horseshoe Bend. The Battle of Horseshoe Bend was another bloodbath. About a thousand Indian warriors, outnumbered by an army with better weapons, were massacred. Three weeks later, the Muskogee Nation surrendered to Jackson.

Muskogee Chief Red Eagle (also known as William Weatherford) surrenders to Andrew Jackson after the Battle of Horseshoe Bend. John Reuben Chapin, 1859.

Acting on authority from President Madison, Jackson forced the Muskogees to sign a treaty ceding twenty-three million acres of Indian lands to the United States—large sections of what is now Alabama and Georgia, a land grab that opened immense tracts of fertile soil to American farmers and land speculators. It was the first of many treaties Jackson would force upon the Muskogees and other tribes. The pattern was always the same. After beating the Indians mercilessly in war, he gave them no choice but to sign a treaty with terms highly favorable to the United States. While Jackson was hailed throughout the United States as a military hero, in the words of one historian, the truth was far less romantic: When provoked, Jackson was a ruthless killer.

7

The Battle of New Orleans

"Some believe me, as they term it, a most dangerous and terrible man—of savage habits & disposition, and wholly unacquainted with civilised life: Possessing a temper and turn of mind of the most incorrigible cast; and that I can break & trample under foot the constitution of the country with . . . unconcern and careless indifference."

—Andrew Jackson

President Madison rewarded Jackson with a commission as major general in the U.S. Army. The British army had recently set fire to the new capital, located now in Washington, D.C., sending the president and his cabinet fleeing to Virginia for safety in the dead of night. American forces stopped the British at Baltimore, but were crumbling before the better equipped and better organized British army. An American delegation journeyed to Europe to enter peace talks with Britain. Because news traveled so slowly, Americans back home had no idea whether the talks were in fact a surrender and the end of the United States, or an honorable settlement.

The British launched ten thousand troops and sixty ships to New Orleans, the largest force Britain had ever turned on the country. Americans feared the worst. Given New Orleans's strategic position at the base of the Mississippi River, a British victory in New Orleans would be disastrous for the United States.

President Madison put Jackson in charge of defending New Orleans. Jackson arrived in the city and set to work putting together what has been called a motley army. He started

MARTIAL LAW, OR MILITARY RULE, is when a military takes over the government, suspending ordinary laws and imposing its own laws. *Civil liberties* refer to the rights of individuals to be free from a tyrannical or unjust government, including military rule. One of the many protections in the United States Constitution against loss of civil liberty at the hands of the government is the writ of habeas corpus. Habeas corpus is Latin for "you shall have the body," and refers to the government summoning a person for questioning or holding a person without a trial. The writ with seven hundred men he had brought from Tennessee, and added a band of pirates from the Caribbean who wanted the British navy out of their waters. Soon an old friend, General John Coffee, arrived with about six hundred soldiers. The next day, fourteen hundred Tennessee recruits marched into New Orleans. Even with the arrival of an additional two thousand Kentucky militiamen, many of whom were expert marksmen, the Americans were gravely outnumbered against a better trained adversary. When many of the Kentucky militiamen arrived without guns, Jackson quipped that it was the first time he'd seen a

of habeas corpus allows citizens to appeal to a court of law if they feel that they are being detained unjustly. Article 1, Section 9 of the Constitution provides that, "The Privilege of the Writ of Habeas Corpus shall not be suspended, unless when in Cases of Rebellion or Invasion the public Safety may require it." Because Article 1 outlines the powers of the legislature, and because allowing the army to suspend civilian rights would permit military rule, legal scholars now and in Jackson's time understand that only Congress has the power to suspend the writ of habeas corpus.

Kentuckian without "a jug of whiskey, a pack of cards, and a gun."

Jackson received warnings from Governor William Charles Cole Claiborne and others within the city that enemies of the United States lurked in New Orleans, men still loyal to Britain or Spain. Jackson agreed. "We have more dread from spies and traitors, than from open enemies," he wrote to Claiborne. Jackson wasn't about to take any chances—and he wasn't one to quibble over fine points of the law. He declared martial law in New Orleans, placing the entire city under military rule and suspending the writ of habeas corpus.

In a stunning act unprecedented in America's short history, Jackson declared himself the sole ruler of New Orleans. He decreed that all who entered or exited the city must report to him. He ordered all streetlamps to be extinguished at nine PM, and commanded that anyone found on the streets after that hour was to be arrested as a spy. He took possession of slaves, oxen, carts—anything he needed. He forced Indians to serve as foot soldiers. He warned that anyone who disobeyed his orders would be "punished with the utmost severity." Everyone knew that Jackson's threats must be taken seriously. Jackson answered accusations that he was behaving like a tyrant by insisting that he had no choice: Martial law was necessary to root out British spies and keep the city safe.

Jackson entrenched his army at the Rodriguez Canal about six miles downstream from the city. Rodriguez Canal was a dry ditch ten feet wide and four feet deep joining a cypress swamp with the Mississippi River. The Americans reinforced their trench with a breastwork of logs and earth eight feet high by twelve feet thick.

The British arrived, and New Orleans quaked with fear.

For weeks there was sporadic fighting. Numerous escaped slaves fought alongside the British, hoping a British victory would ensure their own liberty. One of the escaped slaves wore a collar of iron bars on his neck devised to prevent him from lying down. A British officer had a blacksmith remove it, sneering

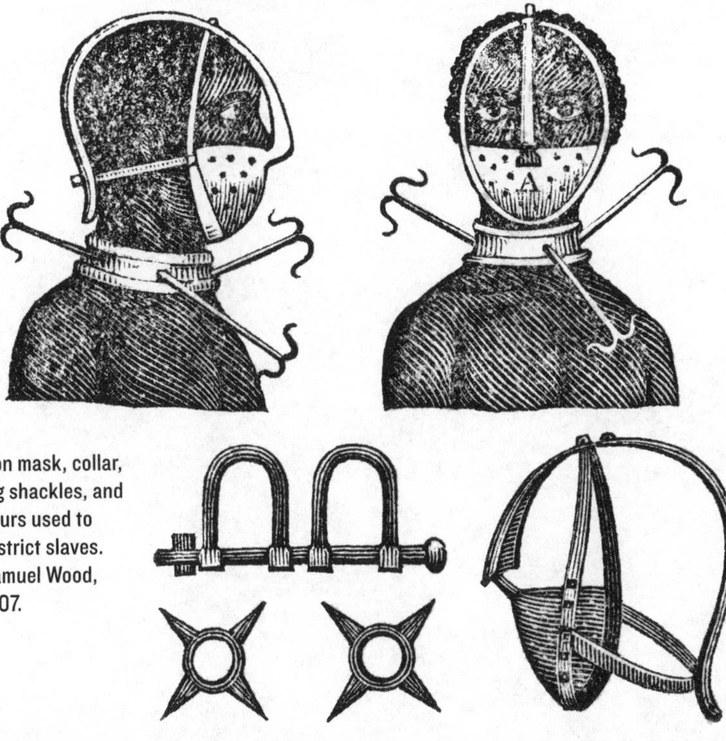

Iron mask, collar, leg shackles, and spurs used to restrict slaves. Samuel Wood, 1807.

over "this ingenious symbol of a land of liberty." There were also blacks fighting on the American side, including free men and those still enslaved on loan by their owners.

The final showdown between the British and Americans, which was later called the Battle of New Orleans, began at about six in the

morning to the beat of drums. An American band played "Yankee Doodle," the notes rising over the thunder of gunfire. British General Edward Michael Pakenham counted on cover from the morning mist, but the mist rose early, giving the American marksmen a clear

View of the Battle of New Orleans, showing British troops advancing across open ground toward the Americans, who were behind earthworks. Illustrates General Packenham mortally wounded and held by his officers, and offers a cameo portrait of General Jackson. Engraved by Francisco Scacki, published between 1815 and 1820.

view of the advancing British. The Kentucky militiamen fired with deadly precision. American canons and a thirty-two-pound naval gun proved even more deadly. After two hours, when the shooting had stopped and the smoke had cleared, the Americans looked over the fortification, stunned by the sight. Heaps of fallen British soldiers stretched out for more than a quarter of a mile. More than fifteen hundred soldiers lay wounded, with hundreds more dead. American casualties totaled thirteen dead and thirty-nine wounded.

The British had no choice but to retreat. Even with the defeated British in retreat, Jackson did not lift his iron control of the city. He ordered so many arrests and imprisonments that New Orleans mayor Nicholas Girod complained that the guardhouse was nearly full, but Jackson continued ordering arrests, claiming that "the enemy are still hovering around us & perhaps mediates an attack."

Later, Jackson learned that prior to the Battle of New Orleans, British and Americans had agreed to end the war in terms that amounted to a stalemate, signing what came to be called the Treaty of Ghent. Because of the slowness of communication across the Atlantic, it took weeks for the news of the treaty to reach the United States. The Battle of New Orleans, fought after the treaty was signed, was not without significance. Many believed that if the British, who never recognized the legality of the Louisiana Purchase, had captured New Orleans, they would have turned the city over to the Spanish.

When word spread of Jackson's victory at New Orleans, joy erupted throughout the nation. Jackson had done what no modern nation had been able to do—he fought the mighty British to a standstill. Headlines across the nation blazed Jackson's glory. Congress hailed him as a hero and ordered a special gold medal struck

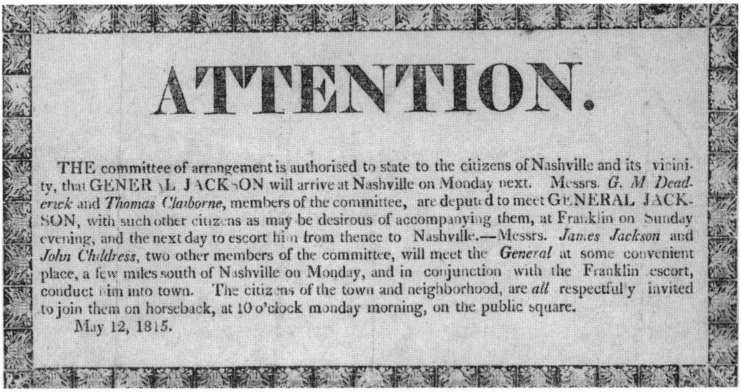

ATTENTION.

THE committee of arrangement is authorised to state to the citizens of Nashville and its vicinity, that GENERAL JACKSON will arrive at Nashville on Monday next. Messrs. *G. M Deaderick* and *Thomas Claiborne*, members of the committee, are deputed to meet GENERAL JACKSON, with such other citizens as may be desirous of accompanying them, at Franklin on Sunday evening, and the next day to escort him from thence to Nashville.—Messrs. *James Jackson* and *John Childress*, two other members of the committee, will meet the *General* at some convenient place, a few miles south of Nashville on Monday, and in conjunction with the Franklin escort, conduct him into town. The citizens of the town and neighborhood, are *all* respectfully invited to join them on horseback, at 10 o'clock monday morning, on the public square.

May 12, 1815.

Announcement of Nashville's official welcome for Jackson after the Battle of New Orleans, 1815. Gold medial presented to Jackson by Congress, 1815.

in his honor. Songs were composed commemorating his victory. "His popularity is unbounded," cried one Tennessee newspaper, "old and young speak of him with rapture." In the words of another newspaper, he had restored the nation's faith in itself.

* * * * * * * * * * * * * * *

President Monroe next entrusted Major General Jackson with the task of securing the border with Spanish Florida. Florida, acquired by the Spanish from the British after the American Revolution, had become a haven for runaway slaves. What became known as the First Seminole War began when Jackson attempted to capture runaway slaves living among the Seminole Indians in Florida. If an Indian chief refused to yield to Jackson's dominance, Jackson ordered his army to destroy the village. One Indian village after another lay wasted by his army.

What Jackson did next exceeded his orders. He invaded Spanish strongholds in Florida. Spanish power in the Americas had been crumbling, so he met with little resistance. He seized the Spanish fortress at St. Mary's and torched a Seminole village. In the process, he captured two British subjects in Florida, Robert Ambrister and Alexander Arbuthnot. After a lightning-swift trial, he executed them on charges of stirring up the Seminoles against the United States.

Flush with excitement and victory over his capture of Florida, Jackson wrote to President Madison that if given additional troops, he would capture Cuba and add to "the growing greatness of our nation." What Jackson didn't anticipate was the moral outrage across America sparked by his invasion of Spanish Florida. Bending the rules to defend an American city against the attacking British army had been one thing. Unauthorized conquest of Spanish Florida was another. Jackson was accused of declaring war on Spain without authority of Congress or the president and in clear violation of the Constitution. His executions of two British agents were called brutal killings that served no military purpose but cruel vengeance. Congress opened an investigation into Jackson's crimes.

John Quincy Adams, who was then secretary of state, diplomatically defended Jackson, arguing that he had acted from passionate patriotism and that his conquest of Florida had been a necessary extension of the mission to secure the border. In the wake of Jackson's victory, Adams negotiated an agreement between Spain and the United States, buying Florida for $5 million. Congress reluctantly found Jackson not guilty, but nonetheless ripped him for flagrant disregard of the Constitution.

Jackson, frail and exhausted from the strain of battle, turned down an offer to run for governor of Tennessee. He accepted, though, a request from President Monroe to journey to Florida and serve as temporary governor to supervise the handing over of the territory to the United States. On June 1, 1821, Jackson resigned from the army, hence officially ending his military career. He traveled to Florida with Rachel and Andrew Jr. Rachel didn't like Florida. They arrived in the hottest season, and she was scandalized that the Floridians didn't respect the Sabbath. At Rachel's urging, Jackson imposed strict Protestant Sabbath regulations on the Catholic population.

By the end of the summer, Jackson considered his work finished. He and his traveling party that included Rachel and Andrew Jr. returned to Tennessee. Jackson needed to rest and regain his strength. The bullet Charles Dickinson had fired into his chest caused frequent abscesses near his heart, triggering violent coughing fits and severe bleeding from torn blood vessels. He was fifty-one years old and his teeth had mostly rotted away. He and Rachel both wheezed from smoking, and he had throbbing headaches from too much tobacco chewing. He wanted to build a larger, grander home for Rachel, but he didn't believe he'd live to enjoy the new house. His body had grown so frail he was sure his days were numbered.

He recovered slowly, surrounded by family, friends, former comrades-in-arms, and admirers. As he regained his strength, he enjoyed the life of a Tennessee gentleman: entertaining friends and any important people who visited Nashville, attending horse races, heatedly arguing about politics.

It wasn't long before his name was bandied about as a candidate for president of the United States. When Nashville newspapers hinted at a Jackson candidacy, he never actually said yes, and pretended not to be interested. In the early decades of America's history, the president was supposed to answer the call of the people, not campaign on his own behalf. As his subsequent behavior showed, though, he burned with ambition to be president.

8

The Corrupt Bargain

"John Quincy Adams, who can write.
Andrew Jackson, who can fight."

—a slogan from the 1824 presidential election

The millions of acres Jackson seized from the Indians were fertile and perfect for cotton growing, creating a bonanza of land purchasing and speculating. Alabama, carved out of what was formerly Indian territory, became a state in 1817. Mississippi followed in 1819, naming its capital for Andrew Jackson.

Jackson and those around him cashed in on the land grab. His good friend John Coffee became surveyor general of Alabama, a post that allowed him first pick of prime farmland, which he bought cheap at a government auction. One of Rachel's brothers made a fortune from land speculating. Jackson, too, bought some of the Indian lands. Settlers poured into Mississippi and Alabama, bringing large numbers of slaves. One observer, overcome with shame and disgust by the sight of slaves being marched westward, commented on the "half naked women and men, loaded with chains, without being charged with any crime but being black." Using slave labor, the settlers carved plantations out of the wilderness.

Then, suddenly—to the shock and horror of the nation—the American economy collapsed, causing widespread panic. The nation's first depression was partly triggered by banks making it too easy for settlers and land speculators to borrow money.

Jackson, still feeling the bitter sting of the debt he was saddled with after Allison declared bankruptcy, blamed the crashed economy on evil bankers and the East Coast monied aristocracy who had enriched themselves at the expense of common people.

At the same time, the country was shaken by another political bombshell. In 1819, Missouri had enough settlers to qualify for statehood. When an act was presented to Congress to allow Missouri to draft a state constitution, James Tallmadge, a congressman from Poughkeepsie, New York, proposed that as a condition

THE FIRST BANK OF THE UNITED STATES, established by Alexander Hamilton in 1791 had a twenty-year charter. By the time the charter came up for renewal in 1811, the federal government had fallen firmly in the hands of Thomas Jefferson and his allies. On the grounds that banks were the root of evil and a corruptor of the nation's purity and integrity, they did not renew the charter when it expired, and Hamilton's bank closed its doors forever.

$1,000 promissory note issued by the Second Bank of the United States, 1840

Soon, though, the federal government found itself in financial trouble. The War of 1812 was costly and the federal coffers were becoming depleted. The government therefore established the Second National Bank as a way to finance the war. Proper regulations, though, were not in place, and the bank was incompetently managed. Eager to make money, the bank gave out too many loans. Local banks did the same. Credit flowed freely to people who mismanaged their loans, made bad purchases, or borrowed more than they could repay. There were also allegations that bank employees were dipping into funds for their own personal use.

Debt-ridden, large numbers of borrowers, unable to pay, simply stopped making their payments. When banks began running short on funds, people holding bank notes panicked and demanded that the banks make good on the notes. When too many people tried to cash in their notes, banks crashed—unable to meet the demands, they were forced to close their doors, rendering all the notes issued worthless. The failed banks left a path of destruction. Prices fell, rendering crops and manufactured goods worthless. People lost their homes and farms and fell into poverty.

of Missouri statehood, slavery in Missouri must be prohibited. His proposal created a firestorm of debate. Thomas Jefferson, from retirement, understood immediately that a proposal like Tallmadge's could tear the country apart. He said Tallmadge's proposed condition was a "fire bell in the night," which awakened him and filled him with terror. "I have been among the most sanguine in believing that our Union would be of long duration," Jefferson wrote. "I now doubt it much."

Jackson didn't believe the anti-slavery protests were motived by humanitarian impulses. He believed abolitionism was nothing more than political expediency. In his view, Northern industrialists and bankers, who wanted power and thought the South

THE RULE COUNTING EACH SLAVE as three-fifths of a person was the result of a compromise among the drafters of the Constitution. Because each state's number of congressional representatives would be proportional to its population, a dispute arose among the drafters about how to count enslaved people. Many considered enslaved men, women, and children to be property. The South, where slaves vastly outnumbered was too strong, knew that quashing slavery would reduce the South to rubble. Indeed, because of the three-fifths rule, giving Southerners three votes for every five slaves, the South dominated national politics.

Because of the three-fifths rule, of the five presidents who had served so far, four had been Virginians: George Washington, Thomas Jefferson, James Madison, and James Monroe. John Adams—who served only a single term—hailed from Massachusetts. The Virginians each served two terms.

As often happened, the Constitution—which often lends itself to different interpretations—could be marshaled by both sides. Those in favor of Missouri entering as a slave state, viewing

whites, ironically wanted the slaves counted as humans and not property so Southern states would have more power in Congress and the North would not be able to outlaw slavery. The North didn't want the enslaved people to count because if they did, the Southern states would hold a majority even though very few Southerners had a voice in government. The compromise was that each enslaved person counted as three-fifths of a person.

slaves as property, pointed to the Fifth Amendment, which prevented the government from depriving people of their property without due process of law. Pro-slavery defenders argued that nothing in the Constitution gave the federal government the authority to regulate slavery within states or territories. Those opposed to Missouri entering as a slave state also claimed that the Constitution was on their side, pointing to Section 9 of Article 1 of the Constitution, which allowed Congress to regulate the "migration" of slaves after 1808.

The Missouri debate was resolved in what came to be called the Missouri Compromise: To keep the slave and free states balanced, Missouri was admitted as a slave state and Maine as a free state, with slavery forever banned in territories west and north of Missouri. The Missouri Compromise didn't really please anyone. Southerners were angry at the very idea that Congress could make laws regarding slavery, and abolitionists were alarmed that slavery was spreading to the southwest.

★ ★ ★ ★ ★ ★ ★ ★ ★ ★ ★ ★ ★ ★ ★

In 1822, the Tennessee legislature endorsed Jackson for president of the United States for the 1824 presidential election. Then in 1823, in a startling turnabout, the Tennessee legislature elected him to the U.S. Senate. Jackson was stunned—and unhappy. He wanted to be president with the power to make changes. He didn't want to be a senator. For years he'd been railing against Congress as a sewer of corruption in the pockets of bankers and monied elite. But he felt it was his duty to go when summoned to public service, so he said goodbye to Rachel and journeyed to Washington, D.C.

It had been twenty-five years since Jackson had served as Tennessee congressman and senator. As before, Jackson came to the nation's capital with a mission: To protect the rights of slave owners and white settlers. This time, though, he arrived as a national celebrity. He was amused when people met him and, knowing him only by reputation, were shocked to find that he was a perfectly civilized gentleman. He quipped that "I am told the opinion of those whose minds were prepared to see me with a tomahawk in one hand, and a scalping knife in the other."

Jackson made a strong impression when he entered a room, despite the fact that he was now fifty-five with a weakened body. Because of his height, his erect carriage, his shock of white hair, and the sheer strength of his personality, all eyes remained on him. He often spoke quickly and forcibly, shaking a clenched fist to make a point.

In Washington, he met up again with Thomas Benton, Jesse Benton's brother—the one who had fired the bullet into Jackson's shoulder during their frontier brawl, a bullet that remained lodged near his shoulder. He and Benton patched up their differences and found that as fellow representatives from slave states—Benton was now a senator from Missouri—they were on the same side of most issues. Eventually Benton would become one of Jackson's most ardent supporters.

* * * * * * * * * * * * * * *

The 1824 presidential election was drawing near. The four strongest candidates were Andrew Jackson, Henry Clay, William Crawford, and John Quincy Adams, son of former president John Adams. All four were members of Jefferson's Democratic-Republican party and each declared himself the natural heir of Thomas Jefferson. Even Adams, whose father had been a Federalist, had long since declared himself a Democratic-Republican.

John Quincy Adams, engraved by James Barton Longacre, circa 1825

The Corrupt Bargain

DURING George Washington's presidency, the two major parties were the Democratic-Republicans, led by Thomas Jefferson, and the Federalists, led by Alexander Hamilton. The Democratic-Republicans generally stood for states' rights and a small federal government, while the Federalists represented the interests of merchants and industry. The Federalists' support came largely from urban areas and cities while the Democratic-Republicans drew their strength from the rural countryside.

Even before Alexander Hamilton died fighting a duel with Aaron Burr, Hamilton's Federalist Party was in steep decline. After Hamilton's death, Jefferson and the members of his party persuaded a majority of Americans that concentrating power in a federal government would lead to loss of liberty and states' rights. The death knell for the Federalists came when they opposed the War of 1812 and were thus dubbed unpatriotic. By the end of the 1820s, for all practical purposes, the Federalist Party was no longer in existence, leaving only one dominant party—Jefferson's Democratic-Republican Party.

Jackson's chief competition was Secretary of State John Quincy Adams, a highly skilled and widely respected diplomat with an impressive list of credentials. A graduate of Harvard College, he'd held government appointments under President George Washington, President James Madison, and President James Monroe. He was widely respected as a serious, devout, and hardworking intellectual. Because a tradition had arisen that the secretary of state was training grounds for the presidency, many people took for granted that he would become the next president.

Because of Adams's previous support for Jackson when Jackson invaded Florida, and because Jackson's own qualifications and education were thin, Adams expected Jackson to accept the position of his vice president. But Jackson was not interested. He had no desire to play second fiddle.

Initially, Adams and his supporters didn't take Jackson seriously. They expected voters to see the danger in elevating to the presidency a military leader with a history of taking the law into his own hands. Indeed, many of Adams's contemporaries saw Jackson as a modern-day Julius Caesar—the Roman military hero who made himself a dictator and brought about the downfall of a great republic. Thomas Jefferson summed up the attitude of many toward Jackson as a possible president when he said, "He is one of the most unfit men I know of for such a place . . . he is a dangerous man."

But Jackson was wildly popular, particularly in the South and along the frontier, as the hero of the Battle of New Orleans and the general who had quelled the Indian threat and opened the West to white settlers. He was a popular symbol of patriotism second only to George Washington. With his reputation as a fierce fighter and hatred of banks and the monied elite, his candidacy caught fire with the disaffected of the nation—people who felt left behind in the industrial boom and the farmers, plantation owners, and frontiersman who didn't think the government protected their interests.

Unlike today, when all voters go to the polls on the same day, in Jackson's time different states voted at different times throughout the fall with the last ballots cast in November. Then it took several weeks for the votes to be counted and the results carried to Washington, D.C., for the final tally. When the votes were counted, Jackson received the most votes with 42 percent of the popular vote. Adams was next with 31.5 percent. Clay and Crawford both received 13 percent. No candidate received a majority of electoral votes.

ELECTIONS THEN, AS NOW, were decided through the electoral college, a complex system of delegates selected by the states: The states elected their delegates to the electoral college, who then elected the president. Today, while nothing in the Constitution or federal law governs how electoral delegates vote, state laws and political parties generally require them to vote according to the popular vote in their state.

Without an electoral majority, under the Twelfth Amendment of the Constitution, it was up to the House of Representatives to select a president from the three candidates with the highest electoral count. Henry Clay received the fewest electoral votes, so he was dropped from the list of contenders. Clay, however, was then serving as Speaker of the House, a position that gave him enormous power over the selection of the next president.

✶ ✶ ✶ ✶ ✶ ✶ ✶ ✶ ✶ ✶ ✶ ✶ ✶ ✶ ✶

On a fateful Sunday evening, Henry Clay and John Quincy Adams spent three hours together in Adams's library. They talked about the future of the country. According to a note

Adams made in his diary, Clay asked Adams to "satisfy him with regard to some principles of great public importance, but without any personal considerations for himself." Clay and Adams had long been political rivals, but came together now in a desire to prevent Jackson from becoming president.

Henry Clay, by Charles Bird King, artist, and Peter Maverick, engraver, 1822

Henry Clay agreed with Jefferson's assessment of Jackson. He believed elevating Jackson to the presidency would "give the strongest guarantee that the republic will march in the fatal road which has conducted every other republic to ruin."

One historian concluded that the meeting between Clay and Adams had been primarily to smooth over their differences. After the meeting, Clay threw his support behind Adams. As a result of Clay's influence, the House of Representatives selected Adams as president with John C. Calhoun of Kentucky as his vice president. Five days later, Adams appointed Henry Clay secretary of state.

Jackson and his supporters were enraged. Jackson accused Adams and Clay of striking a corrupt bargain. "This, to my mind, is the most open, daring corruption that has ever shown itself under our government," Jackson wrote. "I weep for the liberty of my country . . . the rights of the people have been bartered for promise of office." Jackson tended to see conspiracies everywhere, and he became convinced that the Adams-Clay alliance was part of an actual long-running conspiracy of the elite northeastern aristocracy to steal power from the people.

There was some irony in Jackson's accusation that what Adams and Clay did was corrupt given his own history of playing politics and accepting jobs from friends. In 1788, Jackson had benefitted when his friend John McNairy, the newly appointed judge of Davidson County, handed out jobs to his friends, including giving the job of prosecuting attorney to Jackson. When Jackson wanted to be major general of Tennessee, he'd had no qualms about exchanging favors with then-governor Archibald Roane. Nor did Jackson see a problem with himself and his family cashing in on the land taken from the Indians by means of family and political connections.

Jackson's defenders claimed that the Clay and Adams bargain was corrupt because they had overturned the will of the people—which was true. Jackson was the popular choice. On the other hand, Clay and Adams had followed the Constitution to the letter.

Clay and Adams denied they'd struck any kind of

bargain—they insisted the House simply selected the man they believed most qualified, which was precisely what they were supposed to do. The accusation that Adams and Clay had struck a corrupt bargain turned out to be devastating. Adams and Clay were both damaged politically and forever lost credibility with the public. The economic crisis and failure of the banks had already shaken faith in the federal government. When Jackson and his followers cast the bargain between Clay and Adams as two members of the ruling elite trying to protect their privilege, confidence in the federal government eroded further.

After attending Adams's inauguration, Jackson voted in the Senate against Clay's appointment. Once Adams and Clay were in power as president and secretary of state, Jackson resigned his seat in the Senate and returned to Tennessee to prepare for the 1828 presidential election. George Washington had disliked political parties and said that after an election, the people should come together for the good of the country no matter who wins. Jackson was having none of that. He was not one to accept defeat, ever, under any circumstances. He was not about to surrender gracefully, particularly under circumstances in which he felt that he—and the will of the people—had been corruptly thwarted. He intended to bring down both Clay and Adams.

PRESIDENCY!!!

This is the House that We' built.

TREASURY.

This is the malt that lay in the House that WE Built,

John Q. Adams,

This is the *MAIDEN* all forlorn, who worried herself from night till morn, to enter the House that We built.

CLAY,

This is the *MAN* all tattered and torn, who courted the maiden all forlorn, who worried herself from night till morn to enter the House that We built

WEBSTER,

This is the *PRIEST*, all shaven and shorn, that married the man all tattered and torn, unto the maiden all forlorn, who worried herself from night till morn, to enter the House that We Built

CONGRESS,

This is the **BEAST**, that carried the Priest all shaven and shorn, who married the man all tattered and torn, unto the maiden all forlorn who worried herself from night till morn, to enter the House that We Built.

CABINET,

These are the ***Rats*** that pulled off their hats, and joined the Beast that carried the Priest all shaven and shorn, who married the man all tattered and torn unto the maiden all forlorn who worried herself from night till morn to enter the House that We built

"OLD HICKORY,"

This is the *Wood*, well season'd and good, WE will use as a rod to whip out the RATS, that pulled off their hats and joined the Beast that carried the Priest all shaven and shorn who married the man all tattered and torn, unto the maiden all forlorn, who worried herself from night till morn, to enter the House that We Built

NEW-YORK.

This is the *state*, both early and late, that will strengthen the Wood well seasoned and good, to be used as a rod to whip out Rats that pulled off their hats, and joined the beast that carried the Priest all shaven and shorn, who married the man all tattered and torn unto the maiden all forlorn, who worried herself from night till morn to enter the House that WE Built.

EBONY & TOPAZ

**The People*

9

Demagogue or Passionate Patriot?

"Fear not, the people may be deluded for a moment, but cannot be corrupted."

—Andrew Jackson

Adams was still in the first year of his presidency when the Tennessee legislature passed a resolution calling on the American people to elect Andrew Jackson as the next president. For the next three years, Jackson's supporters made sure the phrase "corrupt bargain" remained in the newspapers, insisting that if the people's will could be destroyed by a bargain between two politicians, liberty

Jackson campaign poster mocking his opponents, 1828

itself was in danger. They claimed that only Jackson, a political outsider, could clean up the rampant corruption in Washington.

Determined to make the Adams presidency a failure, Jackson's supporters opposed Adams at every turn. When Adams suggested a canal-building project, a national university, and an observatory to study the heavens, Jackson's supporters ridiculed the scheme to waste money on "lighthouses in the sky." When President Adams tried to organize an international conference with the newly independent South and Latin American countries, the pro-slavery South, aghast that the new countries prohibited slavery, undermined his efforts. Adams next came into conflict with the governor of Georgia, who wanted to remove the Cherokees from his state. Adams stood firm against the forced removal of Indians, incurring the wrath of Southerners and settlers along the frontier. Adams put forward a public spending proposal to improve roads and communication, but was again shot down by Southerners who believed that such proposals would benefit the industrial North.

The Democratic-Republican party splintered into two factions. The faction headed by Adams called themselves the National Republicans, and the rival faction headed by Jackson called themselves the Democratic Republicans, which they later shortened to the Democrats.

The National Republicans were in favor of the federal government empowering a range of industries. They wanted to improve the country through such programs as building roads and canals. Henry Clay had developed a proposal called the American System: an economic system of tariffs and a national bank with federal funds to build railroads and other internal improvements. The theory behind the American System was that a diverse economy including factories and banks would liberate the nation from dependence on foreign nations. The slogan of the National Republicans was *liberty is power*.

The democrats, in contrast, stood for states' rights, limited federal government, and a promise to support agriculture and small farmers. Jackson considered the American System to be nothing more than Federalism in disguise. Just when it looked like the Federalist Party had at last been stamped out along with the Federalist idea that a strong federal government should promote the interests of industry and banking, here was John Quincy Adams, talking just like Alexander Hamilton. It was no surprise, of course. Adams's father, the first President Adams, had been a Federalist.

During the first year of Adams's presidency, the Marquis de Lafayette, an aging hero of the American Revolution, visited the United States. Many credited Lafayette with helping the United

THE JACKSONIAN DEMOCRATIC PARTY eventually shortened its name to the Democrats, a party still in existence today as one of America's two major parties. Democrats of the twenty-first century, however, bear almost nothing in common with the Democrats of Jackson's era. The Jacksonian Democrats became the party of the South and the Confederacy. During the first part of the twentieth century, the Democrats supported the Ku Klux Klan, white supremacy, and Jim Crow laws. After Democratic president Franklin D. Roosevelt expanded the federal government through major spending programs, and Democrats John F. Kennedy and Lyndon B. Johnson

States win the Revolutionary War by bringing in the French on the side of the colonies. Everywhere Lafayette went, he was greeted with fanfare—cannon salutes and wildly cheering crowds. He was entertained in style by the dignitaries of the nation. On May 4, 1825, he arrived in Nashville for a two-day visit. He stayed at the Hermitage, one of the few private homes where he was entertained.

The following year, on July Fourth—as America celebrated fifty years of independence—both John Adams and Thomas Jefferson supported the Civil Rights Act, guaranteeing certain rights to minorities and people of color, there was a great shift in the parties. The Democratic party became the party of civil rights, government programs and regulations, and urban and minority communities. The opposing party, the Republicans—the party of Abraham Lincoln and the Union during the Civil War—morphed slowly into the party of *laissez-faire* economics—which means letting the economy take its own course without government interference. The Republicans also became the party of states' rights, drawing much of their strength from rural, white America.

died quietly in their homes. Adams's final words were "Thomas Jefferson still survives." Among Jefferson's final words, upon waking up from an illness-induced sleep, were to ask, "Is it the fourth?"

The passing of the Revolutionary generation and the patriotism stirred by Lafayette's visit allowed Jackson's supporters to drum up enthusiasm for Jackson, who, after all, carried an actual scar on his head from the Revolutionary War. Jackson believed the Revolutionary War had been fought to elevate the sovereignty

THE FOUNDING FATHERS set up a *republic*, not a democracy. In a pure democracy, each person has one vote, and whatever the majority wants, the majority gets. A republic means that offices of state are elected or appointed rather than inherited. In a republic, the people vote for their leaders, who then govern in the name of the people.

In creating a republic and not a democracy, framers of the Constitution put limits on what the majority could do on the theory that without limits, there would be nothing to stop the majority from passing laws that brutalized the minority—a concept President John Adams called the tyranny of the majority. The Founding Fathers were particularly worried about the dangers of a demagogue—a leader who comes to power through lies and distortions and appealing to darker emotions like fear and prejudice. The founders, members of the Enlightenment who had studied the ancient philosophers, were aware of Plato's warning that the danger with democracy was that anyone who could con a large enough group of people to vote for him could grab power. Too much democracy could lead to mob rule—a frightening prospect and one the Constitution was designed to prevent. In fact, the very word "democracy" for many of the Founding Fathers carried negative connotations of anarchy, chaos, the trampling of minority rights, and decisions made in fear and ignorance.

Alexander Hamilton, in fact, once said that the very purpose of government was to constrain unruly passions and force the people to conform to the dictates of reason. To guard against the tyranny of the majority, the founders created a careful system of checks and balances. One was that any law passed by Congress had to comport with the Constitution, including the guarantees of civil liberties. Another check was that federal judges were appointed for life, and were thus free to exercise independent judgment without worrying about public opinion. Another protection from too much democracy was the electoral college, intended to allow educated men to overrule a disastrous popular choice.

Jackson, on the other hand, had full confidence that the majority would always do what was right. He believed that the will of the majority should not be constrained in any way.

of the people, and for him that meant majority rule. He wanted a common frontiersman's voice to be absolutely equal to the voice of a wealthy New York banker. "I have great confidence in the virtue of a great majority of the people," Jackson said, "and I cannot fear the result." While he understood that the Constitution didn't allow for rule of the majority, he believed that the intention behind the Constitution was to "secure to every man equal rights & privileges." He therefore believed that the Constitution should be amended to allow for majority rule in all matters.

In championing the common people against the educated elite and powerful bankers, Jackson saw himself as defending the oppressed and defenseless. He set out to give true meaning to the phrase *We the People*. He wanted the will of the people to prevail in all matters. To this end, he wanted to get rid of the electoral college. He wanted federal judges to serve limited terms so that they would heed to the will of the majority.

For Jackson, the *people* were male and white.

Jackson's gift for high-flown rhetoric and stirring language allowed him to whip his supporters into a frenzy, stoking fears of greedy bankers and industrialists and corruption in the federal government, which he, the champion of the common man, promised to fix. Given deep-seated fears and prejudice in the nation, it wasn't hard for Jackson to rile people up. Davy Crockett explained that he had grown up being taught to see "the people of New England as a selfish, cunning set of fellows that . . . raised up manufacturers to keep down the South and West."

Whether Jackson was seen as a demagogue or a passionate patriot depended entirely on the individual's worldview. Those who saw value in a national bank and believed any problems came from human error or sheer incompetence or lack of adequate regulations, believed Jackson was claiming there was corruption when there wasn't. Senator Daniel Webster, bewildered, remarked that people genuinely believed that Jackson was about to rescue them from impending disaster.

On the other hand, people who distrusted everything about the federal government and who were suspicious of banking and finance saw Jackson as a defender of the common people against the monied aristocracy. Southerners who lived in fear of slave uprisings and feared the federal government would encroach on their freedom to own slaves saw Jackson as the defender of constitutional liberties. Jackson himself believed that he was trying to bring the country back to the principles upon which the Constitution had been formed—and his admirers agreed.

A New York lawyer, Martin Van Buren, who became one of

Jackson's staunchest supporters, took on the role of what today we would call campaign manager. He was so shrewd a politician that he was called the Little Magician. He knew just how to appeal to the voters. During the decades since the Revolutionary War, the number of people eligible to vote had been dramatically increasing. The Founding Fathers had assumed that the government would remain mostly in the hands of white, educated, landowning men on the theory that a person with a stake in government could be trusted to vote wisely, and on the theory that a man who owned property could exercise independent judgment because he didn't answer to a master or superior. During the decades since the ratification of the Constitution, the states had been gradually expanding voting rights to all white men regardless of whether they owned property.

Martin Van Buren created the first modern campaign. To reach the thousands of new voters, he organized field offices throughout the nation, holding mass meetings and rallies featuring fireworks, rousing speeches, and crowd-pleasing thirty-gallon barrels of whiskey with Andrew Jackson's name emblazoned on them. He advised Jackson to avoid getting bogged down in policy details and instead to talk about democracy, the people, liberty, and rooting out corruption. Among Van Buren's strategies was for

Jackson to avoid mentioning slavery, which was rapidly becoming a source of bitterness and passionate arguments.

Jackson, now sixty years old, had no interest in taking the stage himself. He was afraid of falling into a trap and saying the wrong thing. Also, he sometimes had difficulty speaking in public because he had lost so many of his teeth and had trouble with his dentures. Instead, from the Hermitage, he met quietly with supporters, directed his campaign, and wrote letters intended for publication in the newspapers.

Jackson's supporters managed to turn Adams's qualifications against him, implying that Adams was an out-of-touch intellectual. Jackson, meanwhile, as a man of the people, could understand the needs and fears of America. Thus began a tradition in politics of candidates with less education running as ordinary Americans, painting their more scholarly opponents as detached and out-of-touch intellectuals.

Van Buren persuaded Vice President John Calhoun, a Kentuckian, to break his alliance with Adams and join Jackson. Van Buren then convinced Jackson that Calhoun's insider government experience would strengthen Jackson's candidacy and give him more credibility. Calhoun was a powerful defender of slavery, and like Jackson, had been born in the Carolina backcountry.

Jackson hesitated before giving in and selecting Calhoun as his vice president. Jackson—prickly about his reputation and not one to overlook slights or insults—had difficulty overlooking the fact that Calhoun had been among those who had lambasted him for invading Florida. Moreover, as a young congressman, Calhoun had been in favor of establishing the Second Bank of the United States, and he'd once proposed a national network of roads and canals—both very Hamiltonian ideas. Jackson wasn't completely convinced that Calhoun was trustworthy, but he had faith in Van Buren's political instincts.

Jackson's supporters established a string of newspapers to advance his candidacy, publishing a stream of attacks on President Adams. Henry Clay, working on behalf of Adams, established a rival newspaper, *Truth's Advocate and Monthly Anti-Jackson Expositor*. Clay's paper printed the stories of how Jackson had summarily ordered the execution of eighteen-year-old John Woods, how he had killed Dickinson in cold blood, and how he had imposed martial law in New Orleans in the spirit of a tyrant. Stories went further back into his youth, painting him as a gambler and spendthrift. The National Republicans circulated ugly handbills featuring a row of coffins and telling the bloody deeds of Jackson.

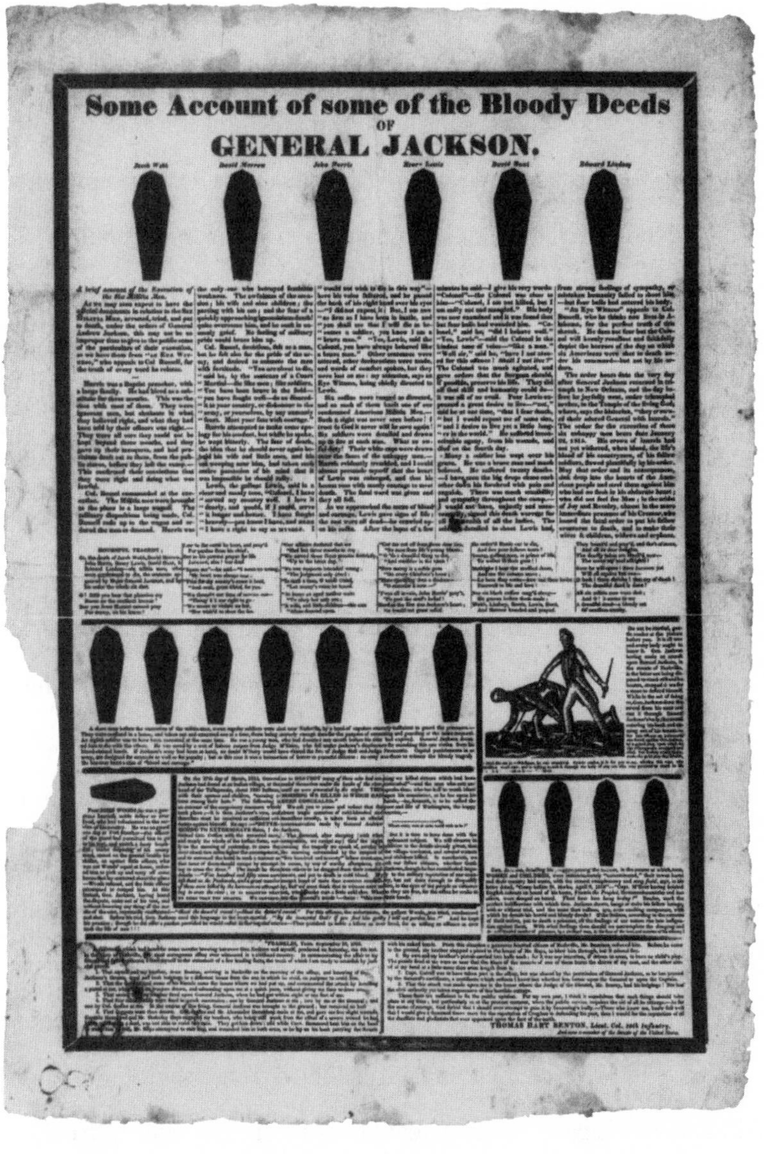

Some Account of some of the Bloody Deeds
OF
GENERAL JACKSON.

Coffin handbill showing the BLOODY DEEDS OF GENERAL JACKSON, 1832

Clay's newspaper investigated the story of Jackson's marriage and dug up the long-forgotten story of Rachel's first marriage to Lewis Robards and how she and Jackson had run off together to Natchez and returned as man and wife. The newspaper called Rachel a bigamist and accused Jackson of running off with another man's wife. Rachel was devastated by the accusations. Had she and Jackson lived the remainder of their lives quietly in Tennessee, nobody would have cared how their marriage had begun. But times changed, and what had been acceptable on the frontier in the late eighteenth century was not acceptable thirty years later to the general American public.

To counter accusations of adultery and bigamy, Jackson's allies invented a dramatic story, which went like this: Rachel fled to Natchez to hide from the violent Robards, with Jackson and several other men traveling along as bodyguards. After depositing Rachel safely in Natchez with family friends, Jackson returned to Tennessee. Shortly after his arrival, Robards sent word that he'd secured a divorce. Overjoyed, Jackson hurried back to Natchez to tell Rachel the good news. He and Rachel got married in Natchez and returned to Tennessee, believing themselves legally wed. A few years later—according to this story—Rachel and Jackson were shocked to learn that Robards had never actually secured a divorce. Instead he'd merely filed for divorce, but lacked evidence that Rachel was unfaithful. So, in an elaborate ruse, Robards fooled Jackson and Rachel into thinking he'd gotten a divorce so that they would begin living together, thus giving him the evidence he needed to obtain the divorce.

Jackson's friend and business partner, John Overton, elaborated on the story by explaining that when Jackson and Rachel learned that there had never actually been a divorce and that their marriage was invalid, he urged them to say their vows again in a small private ceremony, but Jackson resisted, believing that a second ceremony would be akin to an admission of fault. But Overton persisted, and at last Jackson and Rachel agreed to say their vows once more.

Jackson's enemies easily poked holes in this story. Nobody could find evidence of a marriage ceremony in Natchez or Nashville, and there were discrepancies in the dates. Besides, it was preposterous to think that Jackson believed Robards had gotten a divorce almost instantly when divorces were rarely granted, or that Jackson never bothered to check the truth of such an outrageous story. Nobody believed that Jackson accompanied Rachel to Natchez as nothing more than a bodyguard. Jackson was never able to offer any documentary proof to back up this story, not even a marriage license. Even for those who believed Jackson's story, the fact remained that Rachel and Jackson began their relationship before Robards obtained his divorce. As a result, Jackson's political enemies had much ammunition to hurl at him.

The attacks on Rachel enraged Jackson. In his view, slandering a woman was the lowest of the low. When some of his supporters wanted to launch an attack against First Lady Louise Adams, he put his foot down, declaring that he would never make war on females.

There wasn't much mud to throw at the staid and proper Adams, so the Jackson crowd made things up. They spread an outrageous story that Adams had arranged prostitutes for the czar during his service as U.S. minister to Russia, and they accused Adams of installing a White House billiard table at the public expense. Given Jackson's history of duels and executions, one of the more bizarre accusations Jackson's supporters leveled against the bookish and proper Adams was that Adams was an assassin.

The Jackson haters, too, invented outrageous slanders. One Washington, D.C., newspaper declared that:

> General Jackson's mother was a COMMON PROSTITUTE brought to this country by British soldiers. She afterwards married a MULATTO with whom she had several children, of which number General JACKSON is one!!!

Enraged by such slanders, Jackson fought even harder. He railed about how government insiders gave jobs to their friends and family members, who often remained in their jobs for life, creating a culture of insider intrigue and entitlement. Jackson called it blatant corruption. His solution was what he called the rotation system: Each incoming president would sweep out all existing government workers and replace them with new people. His suggestion, which was never implemented, was that no government employee would hold his job for longer than four years. His theory was that by rotating government workers, the government would be more democratic, because more people would have the chance to work at a government job. His critics pointed out that a president coming in and firing everyone and replacing all government employees with his own choices was not only undemocratic, it was downright tyrannical.

✶ ✶ ✶ ✶ ✶ ✶ ✶ ✶ ✶ ✶ ✶ ✶ ✶ ✶ ✶

By December all the ballots had been cast, and the votes were counted and tallied. Jackson won with 56 percent of the popular vote and 68 percent of the electoral college. Adams swept New England, the former stronghold of the Federalists, but Jackson won the West and the South, with the exception of New Orleans, which still seethed with resentment over his heavy-handed martial law.

At the age of sixty-one, Andrew Jackson became America's first backwoods president and the first president to rise to office from a childhood of poverty.

Rachel Jackson as she appeared later in her life. Jackson wore a miniature of this painting on a chain around his neck for the rest of his life. Engraved by J. C. Buttre, created 1883 from a painting by Ralph E. W. Earl, circa 1831.

★ ★ ★ ★ ★ ★ ★ ★

Rachel Jackson had no desire to be First Lady. She didn't want to face the people who had slandered her so cruelly during the election. She feared Washington society would sneer at her country manners and clothing. She had grown unfashionably stout, and she enjoyed smoking a pipe. She was happy in Nashville, surrounded by friends and family and an approving public. “I assure you,” she told a friend, “I had rather be a doorkeeper in the House of God than to live in that palace at Washington.” But Jackson had won the election, so she had no choice but to prepare to move to Washington, D.C.

After a long afternoon shopping in Nashville for clothing suitable for a First Lady, she felt unusually tired. She’d been in poor health for some time, tiring easily and wheezing at the slightest exertion. She stopped to rest at a relative’s newspaper office. There she picked up a pamphlet and started reading—about herself. The article hurled the usual accusations that she was an adulteress and bigamist. Overcome with distress, she crouched in the corner and cried.

After that, her health rapidly deteriorated. A few days later, while going about household duties, she felt a stabbing pain in her chest and left arm. Jackson, frantic, called in the doctors. With Jackson constantly at her side, she seemed to regain strength. On the third afternoon after the stabbing pain, she was moved to a nearby chair so that her bed linen could be washed. While in the chair, she experienced a second attack. She collapsed and fell onto the shoulder of her slave Hannah. Jackson desperately tried to revive her, but was unable to.

Jackson blamed her death on the shock she'd felt seeing accusations about her in print. His initial grief gave way to fury at the slanders that he believed killed her. He vowed he would never forgive those who, in his view, had murdered her.

Her funeral was held on December 24, Christmas Eve. Thousands of people flocked to pay their last respects. Every road leading to the Hermitage was choked with mourners, vehicles of every description, men on horseback, women and children on foot. She was buried in her garden, twenty feet from the entrance to the Hermitage. Jackson followed the pall bearers, pale and thin and broken-hearted. "I shall never forget his look of grief," said one onlooker.

On her tombstone were engraved the words, "A being so gentle and so virtuous, slander might wound but could not dishonor."

Emily Donelson, Rachel's niece. During the first years of Jackson's presidency, she acted as First Lady. This was the official White House portrait.

After several weeks of intense mourning, Jackson was ready to journey to Washington, D.C. He traveled with a party that included his son, Andrew Jackson Jr., his nephew Jack Donelson, who would serve as his private secretary, and Jack's twenty-year-old wife, Emily, who would step into Rachel's place as de facto First Lady. Before leaving the Hermitage, Jackson paid a visit to Rachel's grave. Then, with a heavy heart and tears in his eyes, he climbed into the carriage and began his journey to the White House.

10

The Indian Removal Act

"It will be my sincere and constant desire to observe toward the Indian tribes within our limits a just and liberal policy, and to give that humane and considerate attention to their rights and their wants which is consistent with the habits of our Government and the feelings of our people."

—Andrew Jackson

Jackson wanted to re-create in the White House the intimate atmosphere and family hubbub he'd prized at the Hermitage. So he invited lots of people to move in with him: nieces, nephews, cousins of Rachel's, friends. Even Ralph Earl, a painter whom Rachel had favored and who later married one of her nieces, moved in. Jackson's own son, Andrew Jr., returned to Tennessee to manage the Hermitage, but he visited often. White House residents included children, teenagers, young couples, middle-aged friends, and colleagues and supporters who were Jackson's age. Most called him "Uncle Jackson." He saw his role in his family the same way he saw his role as president: He was the passionately devoted father ready to serve and guide. At the same time, he expected his children to obey.

Seeing himself as the people's president, he kept the door to the White House unlocked—anyone wishing to see him could walk right in. Mostly people came to ask for jobs. Government employees came to plead with Jackson not to fire them. Jackson listened to each plea—and then decided. By his bedside, he kept Rachel's Bible—one in which she had marked her favorite passages. He read several each morning.

✶ ✶ ✶ ✶ ✶ ✶ ✶ ✶ ✶ ✶ ✶ ✶ ✶ ✶ ✶

The first task of a new president is to select a cabinet. Jackson—scornful of the ruling elite and the tradition of presidents selecting cabinet members from the East Coast intellectuals—selected friends and supporters. He saw no hypocrisy in appointing his own friends when he'd accused others who had done something similar of corruption. As president, he had been elected by a majority of voters, so he viewed himself as acting in the interests of the people.

Martin Van Buren, by Henry Inman, 1839

The only member of his cabinet with a national reputation was Martin Van Buren, who he appointed secretary of state. He gave a trusted friend, Amos Kendall, the task of auditing the Department of the Treasury. Before long, Kendall uncovered a Treasury employee who had stolen thousands of dollars of federal funds. "Assure my friends," wrote a triumphant Jackson, "we are getting on here well, we labor night and day, and will continue to do so until we destroy all the rats who have been plundering the Treasury." Jackson's auditors found other thieves, too. Before long, after flushing out enough "rats," Jackson reduced expenditures in the Navy Department alone by a million dollars.

Jackson also appointed Samuel Swartwout, a good friend of his with no financial experience, to run the New York customs operation. The busy port of New York was the chief source of income for the new nation. Money collected from goods passing through the port made up half the federal government's income, which meant large sums of money would pass through Swartwout's hands. Van Buren cautioned Jackson against appointing Swartwout, warning him that Swartwout's appointment would "not be in accordance with public sentiment, the interest of the country, or the credit of the administration." Swartwout was a loyal friend, so Jackson appointed him anyway. Swartwout was later caught stealing more than a million dollars in federal money.

It was Jackson's pick for secretary of war, John Eaton, that caused a firestorm. Eaton, a good friend and confidant, had been one of Jackson's key supporters in Tennessee. Jackson once told Rachel that Eaton "is more like a son to me than anything else; I shall as long as I live estimate his worth and friendship with a grateful heart."

The problem was that a few months earlier, Eaton—a middle-aged widower—married a vivacious twenty-nine-year-old beauty named Peggy O'Neal Timberlake, the daughter of a hotel owner, and a woman with a scandalous reputation. For years Peggy was married to a naval officer, but according to Washington, D.C., gossip, when her husband was away, she entertained other men. The gossips insisted that she took up with John Eaton while her husband was still alive. Her husband committed suicide, which set tongues wagging and prompted speculation that his cheating wife had driven him to despair. Washington society was horrified when Peggy married John Eaton shortly after her husband's death without going through a proper period of mourning.

The Washington, D.C., socialites didn't like Peggy and refused to receive her—meaning they would not have her as a guest in their homes and would not socialize with her in any way. Jackson's niece Emily summed up the situation in a letter home to Tennessee when she said of Eaton, "His wife is held in too much abhorrence here ever to be noticed or taken into society."

Before marrying Peggy, Eaton consulted with Jackson. Jackson, who himself had married the girl he loved in questionable circumstances, urged Eaton not to bend to petty gossip, but instead to follow his heart. Jackson had nothing but contempt for the gossip of Washington high society—the same society, after all, that had looked down on him as an uncouth frontier bumpkin.

When the word went around that Jackson intended to appoint John Eaton to his cabinet, a stream of agitated people came to warn Jackson, repeating the stories of Peggy's scandals. Jackson didn't want to hear it. He wasn't about to have his choice of a cabinet member dictated by petty and malicious gossips. The situation heated up when Vice President Calhoun's wife, Floride, refused to be in the same room with Peggy Eaton and persuaded other Washington wives to do the same. By custom, the cabinet members and their wives sat together at state dinners and balls, and the other wives made a fuss by refusing to sit with Peggy Eaton. It made White House social life unbearable. To Jackson, the whole thing was distracting and ridiculous.

To put an end to the problem, Jackson summoned Calhoun and told him that his wife must stop it. Calhoun replied that there was nothing he could do about his wife's behavior. Jackson decided to pay a visit to Calhoun's wife himself. He called on Mrs. Floride Calhoun in her home and entreated with her to stop snubbing Peggy Eaton. She listened calmly. When Jackson finished speaking, she called for the butler and imperiously told her butler to show Jackson—the president of the United States—to the door.

Jackson concluded that it was all part of a plot to humiliate him and bring him down. He believed Calhoun, power hungry and jealous of Eaton, was conspiring to make his life difficult. Once Jackson decided that the entire thing was a conspiracy to bring down his presidency, he threw down the gauntlet: He announced that anyone who snubbed Peggy Eaton was also snubbing him personally. He measured the loyalty of each of his cabinet members by whether or not they were willing to socialize with Peggy Eaton. As a result, Martin Van Buren, who was willing to receive the Eatons, moved high in Jackson's favor, and Calhoun fell from favor altogether.

Meanwhile, trouble was brewing in Georgia. The legislature of Georgia was hell-bent on getting the Cherokees out of their state, not because the Cherokees were causing trouble—they weren't—but because they were sitting on valuable land. Federal treaties had given the Cherokees a 6.2-million-acre homeland that cut a swath through Georgia's most fertile farmland. The Georgia legislature planned to seize the Cherokee land, divide it into parcels, and distribute it to white Georgians through a lottery.

The Cherokees, led by Chief John Ross, mounted a sophisticated resistance. The tribe hired lawyers, wrote a national constitution, and declared themselves a sovereign people under the United States Constitution and treaties. Ross, the son of a Cherokee mother and Scottish father, grew up bicultural and attended a school that accepted Cherokee students. He and Jackson already knew each other. During Jackson's wars against the

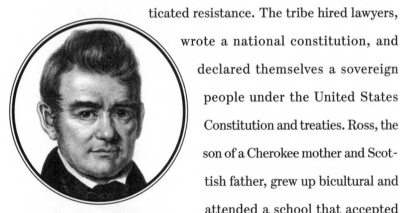

John Ross, Cherokee Chief, as a young man, drawn, printed and colored at the Lithographic and Print Colouring Establishment. Published in *History of the Indian Tribes of North America*, 1842.

Muskogee Indians, John Ross and the Cherokees had fought on his side. In fact, many said that without the help of the Cherokees, Jackson would not have won the Battle of Horseshoe Bend.

A crisis erupted when gold was discovered on Cherokee lands. The nation's first gold rush began on July 22, 1829, with an announcement in the *Georgia Journal* that read, "Two gold mines have just been discovered in this country, and preparations are making to bring these hidden treasures of the earth to use."

Within a few days, thousands of prospectors lusting for gold poured onto Cherokee lands. They came on foot, in wagons, and on horseback. The Georgia legislature declared itself unable to stop the flood of gold seekers. The Cherokee Nation called it the Great Intrusion. One writer in the *Cherokee Phoenix* declared, "Our neighbors who regard no law and pay no respect to the laws of humanity are now reaping a plentiful harvest," and concluded that "we are an abused people."

The Georgia legislature responded by proposing a series of laws making it easier for whites to take Indian lands. On the theory that Georgia law applied to all inhabitants of the state, the law declared the Cherokee Constitution void and made it a crime for the Cherokee Council to meet. Moreover, the law dubbed Indians "nonwhites"—which meant they would not be allowed to vote in Georgia and were considered unfit to testify in courts. This allowed whites to treat Indians any way they chose, and the Indians would have no recourse under the law.

The Georgia legislature was particularly annoyed with missionaries from the North who followed George Washington and John Knox's policy of treating the Indians as sovereign people. Hoping to convert them to American ways, they lived with the Indians on Cherokee lands. The new laws, therefore, made it a crime for any white man to live with the Cherokees without permission from the Georgian government. In passing these laws, the legislature of Georgia made its goal clear: It wanted to drive the Indians out of Georgia.

The Cherokee's argument against the Georgia laws was that under the United States Constitution, they were a sovereign nation and only the federal government had the authority to enter treaties with them. Moreover, the United States, since its inception, had treated the Indians as sovereign people.

But now Jackson was president, and he intended to change that. His understanding of the Constitution was that it did not permit sovereign people to live within the boundaries of the United States. As he saw the situation, the Cherokees had a choice. They could either submit to Georgia law or leave.

THE FIRST AMENDMENT to the Constitution, among other things, protects the rights of people to assemble freely. According to the First Amendment:

> *Congress shall make no law respecting an establishment of religion, or prohibiting the free exercise thereof; or abridging the freedom of speech, or of the press; or the right of the people peaceably to assemble, and to petition the government for a redress of grievances.*

Why then were Georgia's proposed laws—which among other things forbid the Cherokee Council from meeting—not unconstitutional? The hitch was that the First Amendment applied only to laws passed by the *federal* Congress, not state governments. Nothing in the Constitution as it stood in the first part of the nineteenth century prevented states from depriving their own citizens of liberty—which was what made slavery possible.

Jackson believed he was acting humanely and compassionately. He saw himself as the elected father figure of the country who knew what was best for the Indians, who he called his "red children." He made clear his views of the Native Americans in a letter to the Muskogees in 1829 when he wrote: "Friends and Brothers, Listen! Where you are now, you and my white children are too near to each other to live in harmony and peace . . . Beyond the great river Mississippi, where a part of your nation has gone, your father has provided a country large enough for all of you and he advises you to remove to it." He then added the promise, "There your white brothers will not trouble you; they will have no claim to the land, and you can live upon it, you and all your children, as long as the grass grows or the water runs, in peace and plenty. It will be yours forever." Indians understood that the words contained a veiled threat. Go, or suffer continual harassment. Some went. Many resisted.

Four months into Jackson's presidency, Reverend J. M. Campbell, pastor of the Presbyterian church Rachel herself had attended, called on Jackson at the White House. He had come to discuss with Jackson the gossip he had heard about

Peggy. Campbell had heard that, according to a Washington doctor, Peggy had suffered a miscarriage even though her husband had been at sea for one full year.

Jackson responded with unbridled fury. He raged about the depravity of a doctor who would reveal secrets of one of his patients. He insisted that Peggy was innocent, slandered by people who saw themselves as moralists but in fact, were mean and vicious. He was so enraged that "his body shook; his voice cracked." He paced back and forth in front of the frightened Campbell. When Campbell tried to respond, Jackson cut him off saying that, as a Christian preacher, he had an obligation to check the truth of rumors before spreading them. Before the interview ended, Jackson all but ordered Campbell to retract his statements.

On September 10, 1829, in an attempt to resolve the Eaton matter once and for all, Jackson called a cabinet meeting specifically to examine the evidence for and against Peggy Eaton. John Eaton didn't attend. During the meeting, Jackson presented to his cabinet all the evidence against Peggy and roared that she was innocent, behaving as if his cabinet were a court of law that could pronounce Peggy not guilty. He evidently expected his declaration of her innocence to put an end to the matter.

Some cabinet members spoke up either to defend Peggy or to

criticize Eaton. Others, though, sat without moving or speaking, not daring to contradict Jackson to his face. Later, when the word went out about what had happened during the cabinet meeting, many believed Jackson had gone completely mad—calling a meeting of his cabinet to hear evidence of miscarriages and affairs, expecting his judgment to carry the authority of a court of law.

Instead of solving the issue, the meeting led to what was almost a frontier-style brawl. When Peggy Eaton learned that during the cabinet meeting, the secretary of the Treasury, Samuel Ingham, had said unkind things about John Eaton, she insisted that Eaton challenge Ingham to a duel. Ingham declined and begged Jackson to help. Jackson refused to interfere. By Jackson's code of behavior, men fought their own battles. Moreover, if a man insulted another man's wife, he could expect to be called to account. Ingham, terrified, fled from Washington.

Democratic congressmen, embarrassed by the entire thing, issued warnings to Jackson: If things continued this way, they would break from him and the party. Jackson was not about to be bullied by anyone, including congressmen in his own party. He said he would resign his presidency before he would desert a friend like Eaton.

The Indian Removal Act

* * * * * * * * * * * * * * *

In December, Jackson proposed a bill to Congress to set aside lands west of the Mississippi for the relocation of the Cherokees. He asked for federal funds to help with the relocation. He wasn't *forcing* the Cherokees to move, he insisted. He hoped that they would leave on their own.

Jackson's removal bill created an eruption of public protests—a widespread, rancorous public debate in America about equality and what today we call civil rights. Protests against the Indian Removal Act broke out on university campuses, in women's groups, and at town meetings. People circulated petitions pleading for the Indians to be able to remain on their ancestral lands.

The missionaries led the protests, publishing a pamphlet that became one of the most widely read political works during that time in the United States. The Cherokees were, as far as the missionaries were concerned, a model of cultural assimilation. The tribe had entirely adopted American norms and culture. No longer hunters who ranged over the land, they were now settled farmers. They wanted only to remain peacefully on the lands where their ancestors were buried. One missionary paper cried, "Now is the time for every Christian, every philanthropist and every patriot in the United States to be exerting themselves to save a persecuted and defenseless people from ruin." Another predicted that if the Indian Removal Act became law, the Cherokees would become "living monuments of the white man's wrongs."

Jackson called on all Democrats to back him. The Democrats enjoyed a slim but decisive two-vote majority in the Senate, so the Senate therefore approved the bill.

The bill, though, met fierce opposition in the House, led by Senator Theodore Frelinghuysen, who challenged the act as inhumane. Frelinghuysen and others claimed that the Indian Removal Act violated the personal rights of the Cherokees just as slavery mocked the liberty of African Americans. Among those who cried out against Jackson's Indian Removal Act was frontiersman Davy Crockett, who had fought under Jackson's command. Crockett denounced Jackson for persecuting the Southern tribes. Jackson, who took everything personally, never forgave him.

Jackson and his supporters were vexed by the public outcry. Jackson didn't believe that the protests were motived by humane impulses. He believed Northerners just wanted power in the form of a strong federal government meddling in state business and trampling on state autonomy.

Georgia passed another law requiring Indians to pay taxes even though they could not vote. When whites seized Indian property, law enforcement officers stood by and did nothing. The tactics worked. The first of the Southern tribes to give up and move westward were the Mississippi Choctaw. They set off on their journey westward in September of 1830. They marched, hungry and tired. "Death is hourly among us," wrote an army major escorting the Indians westward. "The road is filled with the sick." Later, when the Muskogee Indians departed as well, a writer for the *Montgomery Advertiser* was overcome with pity. "To see a remnant of the once-mighty people fettered and chained together, forced to depart from the land of their fathers into a country unknown to them is . . . sufficient to move the stoutest heart."

John Ross and the Cherokee Nation fought back in the courts. They hired William Wirt, a distinguished attorney, to represent them. They took their case to the United States Supreme Court, asking the Supreme Court to rule Georgia's laws illegal under the Constitution, federal laws, and treaties between the Cherokees and the United States.

The wheels of justice turn slowly. The Cherokees knew it would be months or longer before the Supreme Court handed down its decision. There was nothing to do but wait and endure the harassment of whites who wanted the Cherokee lands.

11

Who Decides?

". . . government being instituted for the happiness and prosperity of the people, all legitimate power must be delegated by them and is necessarily subordinate to them."

—Andrew Jackson

When Congress passed a bill authorizing $150,000 to extend a national highway in Kentucky called the Maysville Turnpike that one day could become part of an interstate highway system, Martin Van Buren advised Jackson to veto it. Van Buren was a strict states' rights Jeffersonian. The last thing he wanted was the federal government building highways. He also believed in letting things take their own course without government interference. He wanted the federal government out of *everything*, including road building. If roads were to be built, let it happen locally. Besides, as Van Buren shrewdly pointed out to Jackson, the road was in Henry Clay's home state of Kentucky.

Jackson vetoed the bill—a startling break with tradition. While the Constitution allowed for presidential vetoes, the Constitution made clear that the Congress passed laws while the president's job was to administer. The presidents who came before Jackson, in an effort to faithfully follow the Constitution, restrained from vetoing Congress's laws.

Jackson—with a bully's instincts about power and how to exploit an adversary's weakness—quickly figured out that brandishing the veto gave him enormous muscle. The ability to say *no* gave him the power to shape laws equal to Congress. After vetoing the highway bill, he vetoed anything he didn't like, quashing more bills than all his six predecessors put together. He justified what appeared to many to be a power grab by explaining that, as president, he had been elected by the people as a whole, so, as the representative of the people, he was obligated to do what he thought was right. His admirers cheered his ability to take control in the name of the people. His enemies accused him of overreaching and invading Congress's territory.

Meanwhile, the Eaton scandal was still percolating. At long last, Martin Van Buren came up with the solution to the Eaton scandal, which he called "this disgusting petticoat business." His idea was for all the members of Jackson's cabinet to resign, including himself. That would give Jackson an excuse to call for a general reorganization of his administration. Jackson could then reassign cabinet members in a way that would remove the Eatons from Washington.

On April 11, 1831, Van Buren put his plan into action. He resigned from the cabinet, and persuaded Eaton to do the same. Once Van Buren and Eaton had resigned, they pressured the others to follow suit. For the first—and last—time in American history, there was a mass resignation from the president's cabinet. The resignations allowed Jackson to shuffle everyone's jobs. Once Jackson finished his reappointments and the shuffle was complete, Eaton had been appointed minister to Spain, taking Peggy with him.

After that, whenever any of Jackson's cabinet members behaved in ways he didn't like or he thought disloyal, he replaced them. Combined with the usual shuffling of offices—men resigning for personal reasons—the door to Jackson's official cabinet seemed to be constantly revolving. Over his time in office, he went through four secretaries of state, five secretaries of the Treasury, three attorneys general, and three secretaries of the navy.

Instead of looking to his official cabinet for advice, Jackson gathered around him an informal group that included friends, family, supporters, and even newspaper editors who agreed with his views. He met regularly with this group for camaraderie and to get advice. In fact, he met with this group more often than he met with his official cabinet. Martin Van Buren was in this group, as was Jackson's nephew Jack Donelson, and a Maryland lawyer named Roger B. Taney. Because the group met with Jackson in the back rooms of the White House, Jackson's critics sneered, dubbing the group the president's Kitchen Cabinet.

With Jackson's body growing feeble—there wasn't a day that passed on which he didn't experience pain—he found comfort in being surrounded by his loyal Kitchen Cabinet and the constant hubbub of extended family. On November 24, 1831, his adopted son, Andrew Jr., married Sarah Yorke in Philadelphia. They named their first child, a girl, for Rachel. With the baby, they moved to the White House, and Sarah Yorke Jackson took on many of the duties that usually fell to the First Lady. Jackson's constant pain and growing feebleness made him think death was near—but ever the fighter, he hung on, believing that he owed the people his service as president.

A TARIFF, also called a customs duty, is a tax paid on certain imports and exports. The purpose of tariffs is to protect domestic industry and manufacturing by driving up the cost of imports, making it less expensive for people to purchase goods that were produced in the country. Imports from Britain were mostly fabric and clothing, so the tariff was intended to protect Northern fabric and clothing manufacturers from British competition, thus promoting American industry.

The problem was that while the tariff benefitted the Northern cloth manufacturers, it harmed the Southern cotton planters. When Congress created the tariff on British imports, the British stopped purchasing as much cotton from South Carolina, and South Carolina was no longer able to purchase inexpensive fabric from Britain.

By 1831, serious trouble was brewing in South Carolina over a tariff. Earlier, during the 1828 campaign, Jackson's supporters—to win support in the North and form a truly national coalition—proposed a tariff on British imports.

During the election of 1824, Jackson supported the tariff with a carefully worded statement intended to please the North while placating the South, a move that allowed Jackson's political enemies to accuse him of being two-faced and deliberately vague, but which brought him much needed Northern support. His campaign reasoned that the South would support him even with the tariff, while Northerners might be brought on board.

In early 1831, Jackson learned that two men had imported goods into South Carolina but refused to pay the tariff on the grounds that it was unconstitutional. The South Carolina government official whose duty it was to collect the tariff went to the federal district attorney for South Carolina and asked him to collect the tax. The federal district attorney also believed that the tax was unconstitutional. He resigned his post so he wouldn't have to collect it.

Jackson himself had approved of the tax, and his supporters had pushed it through Congress, so he took the federal district attorney's refusal to collect the tax as a personal insult and a challenge to his authority. He went so far as to call it treason against the government. His first impulse against the lawbreakers was swift retaliation. He wanted to refuse to accept the federal district lawyer's resignation and to prosecute him for neglecting his duties. But he thought better of the idea. The situation could easily blow up into an armed conflict. A native himself of South Carolina, he understood the people well. He knew he needed to tread carefully. Someone—Jackson suspected his own vice president, Calhoun, also

NULLIFICATION says that any state has the power to void or nullify a federal statute that it believes to be unconstitutional. At first glance nullification appears to be a direct violation of what is known as the Supremacy Clause of the Constitution:

> *This Constitution, and the Laws of the United States which shall be made in Pursuance thereof; and all Treaties made, or which shall be made, under the Authority of the United States, shall be the supreme Law of the Land.*

The Supremacy Clause gives federal laws the power to override state laws. The sticking point is the phrase "laws of the United States *which shall be made in Pursuance thereof*," which says that states are only obligated to follow federal law made *in accordance with* the Constitution.

This raises the question of who decides. Who decides when a law comports with the Constitution? It was a native of South Carolina—wrote and published a document called *Exposition and Protest*, which explained and defined the concept

Calhoun's opinion—and the opinion of many states' rights advocates—that the individual states were allowed to decide for themselves, giving any state the power to ignore any federal statute or treaty it believed violated the Constitution.

The problem, of course, with everyone deciding for themselves is what happens if two states, or two branches of government, disagree? Because the Constitution specifically designates the Supreme Court the arbiter of issues arising under the Constitution, federal laws, and federal treaties, today Americans widely accept the Supreme Court as the final arbiter of Constitutional issues. In the early decades of our nation's history, though, the question was far from decided.

Nullification raised the related question of secession. When the states ratified the Constitution, did they enter into a contract that they were free to leave anytime? Or when states ratified the Constitution, did they forever give up their freedom to secede? The Constitution—vague and sketchy in places—left this question unanswered.

of nullification and called on South Carolina to nullify the tariff.

Jackson understood that if South Carolina nullified the tariff, it would put the United States on the road to breaking apart. He was in favor of states' rights. But nullification? That was where Jackson put his foot down. If a state didn't like a law, they needed to get a majority of American voters on their side and change the law. Nullification would lead to anarchy. If South Carolina could nullify a tax, a Northern state could nullify an act repealing the tax. As Jackson put it, if states could nullify any laws they didn't like, "our country will be like a bag of meal with both ends open. Pick it up in the middle or end wise, and it will run out." His job, as he understood it, was to "tie the bag and save the country."

At a dinner celebrating Thomas Jefferson's birthday, Jackson listened to a series of speeches about the sanctity of states' rights and the rights of states to nullify federal laws they deemed unconstitutional. Jackson then offered a toast. He stood and raised his glass, waiting for others to stand as well and join him. His toast was simple and direct. "Our union," he said. "It must be preserved."

Vice President John Calhoun, by George Peter Alexander Healy, circa 1845

Vice President Calhoun, defiant, responded with his own toast: "The union, next to our liberty, most dear." While Jackson still had no proof that the vice president had authored *Exposition and Protest*, everyone in the room, Jackson included, knew that Calhoun had just declared war on the president.

✶ ✶ ✶ ✶ ✶ ✶ ✶ ✶ ✶ ✶ ✶ ✶ ✶ ✶ ✶

In February of 1832, the United States Supreme Court heard arguments in the case between the Cherokees and Georgia. The State of Georgia claimed that the United States Supreme Court had no jurisdiction over matters that took place within Georgia's borders, so Georgia didn't bother to defend itself in court.

The Supreme Court sided with the Cherokees, declaring Georgia's laws "repugnant to the Constitution, laws, and treaties of the United States" and therefore void.

Georgia ignored the Supreme Court ruling on the grounds that the Supreme Court had no jurisdiction over matters within its borders. Jackson, as president, was supposed to uphold the law and enforce the Supreme Court's decision, but he took no steps to do so. In this case, he believed the Supreme Court was wrong. As Jackson read the Constitution, the Indians had no sovereignty in Georgia.

Jackson believed that as president, *he* was entitled to decide what the Constitution meant. He understood that the Constitution gave the Supreme Court jurisdiction over United States laws, treaties, and the Constitution, but as president he had taken an oath to defend the Constitution. As head of an equal branch of government, he thought his opinion should at least be equal to the Supreme Court.

He actually went further, arguing that, as president, his opinion on Constitutional matters should trump the Supreme Court. His reason? He was elected by the people and represented a majority of voters, while the Supreme Court, with appointed judges serving for life, was the least democratic of the branches, reflecting the

opinion of a small handful of men. John Marshall, the Chief Justice of the Supreme Court and the justice who delivered the decision, had been appointed to the court in 1801 by Federalist president John Adams. Marshall continued to embrace Federalism and the beliefs of George Washington and John Adams, even though—in Jackson's view—the majority of the people had turned against Federalist ideas. Jackson's view was that a man out of touch with the majority of Americans simply should not have so much power.

When Jackson did nothing to enforce the Supreme Court's ruling, Georgia took it as a signal to do as they pleased. Within weeks of the court's decision, Georgia closed Cherokee schools, seized Cherokee farms and land, and distributed them to whites.

Population of an Indian Village Moving, drawn by Theo R. Davis, from *Harper's Weekly*, May 21, 1870

The words to a popular song captured the glee of the whites in seizing Indian lands:

All I want in this creation
Is a pretty girl and a big plantation
Way down yonder in the Cherokee nation.

"We are not safe in our homes. Our people are assailed night and day," a Cherokee leader, John Ridge, wrote to Jackson. Jackson, unmoved, continued to do nothing. Cherokee resistance lasted for years—until, at last, harassed and besieged—they were driven from Georgia. In 1838, the federal government sent seven thousand soldiers to Georgia to steer the Indians west. The soldiers forced Cherokees into stockades at gunpoint while whites looted their homes. The soldiers then marched the Cherokees more than twelve hundred miles to what is now Oklahoma. Historians estimate that more than five thousand Cherokees died along the trail of whooping cough, typhus, dysentery, exhaustion, and starvation. The Cherokees call the road they were forced to walk the Trail of Tears.

12

Jackson's War with the Bank

"[Y]ou know my opinion as to the banks, that is, that the Constitution of our State, as well as the Constitution of the United States prohibited the Establishment of Banks in any state—and that such a thing as loan offices by a State for the purpose of creating a fund out of the property of the State for the payment of individual debts certainly is a power not granted by any provisions of the State constitution, and is unheard of, and prohibited by the principles of general Justice to the people: if even the constitution would permit it."

—Andrew Jackson

In June of 1830, Jackson triumphantly told Congress of his success with Indian removal. "It gives me pleasure to announce to Congress that the benevolent policy of the Government, steadily pursued for nearly thirty years, in relation to the removal of Indians beyond the white settlements is approaching to a happy consummation." That done, he turned his attention to his next task: to destroy Second Bank of the United States. In the same message to Congress he talked of the danger the bank posed to the wellbeing of the nation.

Jackson made clear that reforming the bank wouldn't do. He wanted it shut down entirely—a decision that surprised even many of his own supporters, given how well the bank was then doing. The current director, Nicholas Biddle, appointed by President Monroe in 1819, had pulled the nation out of the depression by expertly and competently administering the bank. Biddle was able to control inflation by regulating interest and credit, which prevented another panic or depression. The bank was performing vital functions: U.S. currency was regulated, the dollar was strong, the federal government had access to credit, the economy was in good shape, prices were stable, and there was an abundance of jobs.

Nicholas Biddle, engraved by John Sartain, 1831

Jackson's enemies claimed he declared war on the bank because of rumors that, during the election of 1828, bank funds had found their way into John Quincy Adams's campaign for president. Jackson's enemies denounced him as petty and vindictive, seeing conspiracies everywhere, destroying anything or anyone that crossed his path. Jackson, however, genuinely believed the bank was unconstitutional and undemocratic, furthering the interests of a British-style monied aristocracy at the expense of the common people. The bank indeed wielded enormous power that would not be permitted today. The bank was a private institution and thus served its own shareholders, but it handled all the federal government's finances, paying its bills and holding its funds. Biddle, as bank president, had a level of power and autonomy unthinkable today. Biddle also made the mistake of arrogantly questioning Jackson's authority over the bank. "No officer of the government, from the President downward, has the least right, the least authority, the least pretense for interference in the concerns of the bank." Biddle's view was that he answered to Congress because Congress had the power to charter a bank or renew the charter.

For Jackson, any political power that didn't result from majority vote was undemocratic and a threat to the wellbeing of the nation. He felt it was his duty as a protector of the people to destroy any seat of power and influence that did not derive its power from majority rule.

Nicolas Biddle, the bank president, also stood for everything Jackson despised. Biddle was the son of a successful Philadelphia merchant. Hailing from a family of staunch Federalists, Biddle was a Princeton graduate and lawyer who had edited a literary journal and served in Pennsylvania's legislature—all before becoming an expert in finance and banking.

Jackson accused Biddle of corruption, of giving bank directorships to people who shared his political views, and of using bank funds to achieve his political ends as a way to keep the monied elite in power. Biddle denied corruption, insisting that he appointed directors because of their qualifications, and that he disbursed funds in keeping with the bank's charter. There was never any evidence that Biddle engaged in illegal activity. But Jackson understood that money was power and Biddle had too much of it.

With the election of 1832 approaching, the National Republicans responded to Jackson's declaration of war on the bank by meeting in Baltimore for one of the nation's first party conventions. They nominated Henry Clay, Jackson's nemesis, for president, and threw their support behind the bank, issuing dire warnings to the nation that if Andrew Jackson was reelected, he would vindictively destroy the bank.

Biddle and the National Republicans devised a bold plan to defeat Jackson in the next election. The bank charter was not due until 1836, but they pushed a charter renewal bill through the House and Senate in January of 1832. The idea was to force Jackson to decide before the election whether to veto the bank bill. They didn't think he'd dare shut down a pillar of the economy in an election year. It would be foolhardy. It would send the economy into a downward spiral, proving for all the world to see that he was a vengeful fool.

Pro-Jackson satire on Jackson's decision to destroy the bank, entitled *Old Jack, the Famous New Orleans Mouser, Clearing Uncle Sam's Barn of Bank and Clay Rats*, by Michael Williams, 1832

The day the bank renewal bill passed both houses of Congress, Nicolas Biddle made an appearance at the Capitol. The applause was deafening and genuinely appreciative. He was, after all, the financial wizard who had snatched the nation from depression. After his appearance at the Capitol, he threw a celebration at his home. The merrymaking went late into the night. Roger Taney, a member of Jackson's Kitchen Cabinet, quipped that the party was loud enough "to make sure it would reach the ears of the President."

* * * * * * * * * * * * * * *

Nicolas Biddle and the National Republicans underestimated Jackson. He viewed their tactics as bullying, and he wasn't about to be bullied.

The Democrats also held their convention in Baltimore—the Democratic party's first nominating convention. They nominated Jackson for president with Martin Van Buren as his vice president.

Eager to make the bank a central issue in the election, Jackson drafted a veto with the help of lawyer Roger Taney and others. The intended audience of the veto was not the Congress, but the people. It was therefore an emotionally charged, rousing document. The veto denounced the bank as a privileged institution that made the rich richer, allowing the monied elite to further their own interests. The veto also declared the bank unconstitutional on the grounds that under the Constitution the federal government did not have the authority to maintain a national bank.

Jackson's claim that the bank was unconstitutional, despite the Supreme Court's ruling, was seen by some as another one of his power grabs. How dare he assume that he had the authority to declare the Supreme Court wrong and to ignore a Supreme Court ruling? Jackson, as always, was polarizing. His supporters applauded him as a truly democratic president, one who wanted the majority to rule in all matters, and that meant wresting control from the Supreme Court, the least democratic branch of government. Jackson's enemies saw him as trying to set himself up as a tyrant.

* * * * * * * * * * * * * * *

To show the people Jackson's ignorance of the basics about banking and commerce and finance, Biddle and Clay published some of Jackson's statements. For example, Jackson once railed against British shareholders of the bank, claiming that allowing the British government to purchase shares in America's bank threatened American autonomy—when everyone with a basic understanding of finance and the bank charter knew

WHEN ALEXANDER HAMILTON proposed the First Bank of the United States, he offered what has come to be called a broad or loose interpretation of the Constitution. Because the Constitution gave Congress power to pass laws that "promote the general welfare," Hamilton argued that Congress had the authority to establish a bank because a bank would promote the general welfare. Thomas Jefferson countered with what has come to be called a strict interpretation, saying that the Constitution said nothing directly about banks, and that reading into the Constitution permission to establish a bank was essentially making things up.

Proponents of a loose interpretation pointed out that viewing the Constitution as ironclad would hinder growth and change, forever freezing the nation as it stood in 1787. Thomas Jefferson, on the other hand, *wanted* the nation frozen as it stood in 1787, when America was essentially a nation of farmers, the economy was agrarian, and states had almost complete autonomy.

Jefferson specifically said that when interpreting the Constitution, people should "carry themselves back" to the time it was adopted and "recollect the spirit manifested in the debates." Critics of Jefferson's approach argued that the Founding Fathers did not speak with a single voice or hold a single opinion, so there was no single intention behind the words and phrases. Besides, there were many who had no desire to freeze the nation as it stood in 1787, when privileged white men ruled and others had few or no rights.

In 1818, after Congress had chartered the Second Bank of the United States, a group in Maryland challenged the bank's constitutionality and took their case to the United States Supreme Court in a case called *McCulloch v. Maryland*. Chief Justice John Marshall, writing for the Supreme Court, followed Alexander Hamilton's interpretation of the Constitution, finding the federal bank constitutional on the grounds that the Constitution gave Congress broad powers to make all laws "necessary and proper" to carry out its duties.

that foreign governments had no vote or voice in the bank, and that being able to use foreign money in American investments helped America.

But Henry Clay and Nicholas Biddle didn't understand the voters the way Jackson did. Most people knew less about banks and finance than Jackson and didn't care about the details. Jackson succeeded in making the bank a symbol of monied aristocracy and corruption and presenting himself as the warrior fighting on behalf of the common man.

The lines were clearly drawn. If Andrew Jackson won reelection, the Second Bank of the United States would go out of existence. Many members of the Washington, D.C., political class expected Jackson to lose. Jackson, though, was confident of victory.

13

Nullification

"I draw a wide difference between States Rights and the advocates of them, and a nullifier. One will preserve the union of States. The other will dissolve the union by destroying the constitution by acts unauthorized in it."

—Andrew Jackson

In July, the same month Jackson vetoed the bank renewal bill, he approved a modification of the tariff that had so irritated South Carolina. The modification reduced South Carolina's tax burden. Jackson saw this as a reasonable compromise: Keep the tariff to protect American industry, but lower it so that the South was not hit as hard. The bill had the support of all the Northern representatives and half of the Southerners.

Many in South Carolina, though, remained rebellious,

claiming that the federal government had no authority to collect taxes in South Carolina. Following the arguments John C. Calhoun outlined in *Exposition and Protest*, militants in South Carolina claimed they didn't have to follow any laws that were unconstitutional—and that South Carolina had the authority to decide what was constitutional within its borders.

* * * * * * * * * * * * * * *

It was thus in a suspended state of crisis that the voters went to the polls in 1832: South Carolina was on the verge of seceding from the Union, and the President was about to kill the Second Bank of the United States.

When the votes were counted, Jackson won 55 percent of the popular vote, and 219 electoral votes to Clay's 49—a stunning landslide. After Clay's loss, the Kentucky legislature elected him as a United States senator. The election wasn't a complete victory for Jackson, though. The election also handed the National Republicans a majority in the senate.

* * * * * * * * * * * * * * *

Seven days after the votes were counted, on November 24, 1833, the South Carolina legislature nullified the tariff on the grounds that it was unconstitutional, declaring that as of February 1, 1834, it would refuse to pay. If the federal government attempted to use force to collect the tariff, South Carolina would secede from the Union.

This defiance shocked and infuriated Jackson, who believed his compromise was perfectly reasonable. If anyone in South Carolina thought that Jackson, who after all had been born in the Waxhaws, would sympathize with them, they were mistaken. Jackson paced through the White House corridors, uttering savage threats against South Carolina. He called in his most trusted advisors, his Kitchen Cabinet, and sat down to hammer out a response. With their help, he drafted a carefully worded proclamation to the people of South Carolina, slamming the nullification theory as absurd and inconsistent with the Constitution. At one point, one of his Kitchen Cabinet members wanted him to rewrite a passage that might offend the states' rights advocates as being too soft on the issue. Jackson bristled and insisted that he write what he believed, regardless of who it offended—one of the many incidents that added to his reputation as a man who stuck by his principles no matter what.

When the proclamation was published on December 10, it

contained the core of his philosophy that the people were sovereign and the Union was perpetual. To argue that states could simply decide to ignore a federal law or secede because they didn't like it, "reduces everything to anarchy & strikes at the very existence of society."

South Carolina responded by preparing for civil war. John C. Calhoun, still vice president until the inauguration in March, resigned and returned home. South Carolina's senator Robert Hayne had been elected governor of South Carolina. He resigned his Senate seat to assume the governorship. In his inaugural address, he threatened war "if the sacred soil of Carolina should be polluted by the footsteps of the invader." Rebels in Charleston stockpiled ammunition and weapons. Volunteer soldiers drilled.

When Jackson learned that South Carolina had struck medals with the inscription, "John C. Calhoun, First President of the Southern Confederacy," he characteristically viewed the whole thing as a conspiracy against him personally. He believed that when Calhoun realized that he would not succeed Jackson as president, he stirred up the whole tariff nullification crisis as a way to grab power. He denounced Calhoun as a traitor and personal enemy. When Jackson learned that South Carolinian ships, in protest, were flying the American flag upside down, he declared that the ships should be sunk for such an outrage against the Union.

Jackson warned a South Carolina congressman that "if one drop of blood be shed there in defiance of the laws of the United States, I will hang the first man of them I can get my hands on to the first tree I can find." The congressman later asked Senator Benton—the same Benton who had once fought with Jackson in a Tennessee brawl—"I don't think he would really hang anybody, do you?" Benton replied that when Jackson talks about hanging, people can begin looking for the rope.

On the issue of nullification, Jackson had widespread support for his position. The entire North was with him, including his political nemesis, Henry Clay. Because the issue was not slavery, most of the South was with him as well.

Jackson again turned to his Kitchen Cabinet to forge a solution. The idea was to issue both a credible threat and a way for South Carolina to back down and save face.

With help from Henry Clay, Jackson pushed two bills through Congress. The first bill further reduced the tariffs by chopping them in half. The second, called the Force Bill, authorized Jackson to use military force to collect the tariffs. Jackson signed both bills into law on March 2. Meanwhile, Jackson prepared for war. He asked for inventories of ammunition and the readiness of soldiers, and assessed federal forts in South Carolina.

The plan worked. On March 15, 1833, Jackson's sixty-sixth birthday, South Carolina backed down. They repealed their tariff nullification bill. After repealing their tariff nullification bill, they also nullified Jackson's Force Bill. Because the Force Bill was rendered unnecessary after South Carolina repealed their tariff nullification bill, the gesture was twofold. It allowed South Carolina to save face, and it allowed them to make the political point that they believed they were entitled to ignore any federal laws they didn't like.

Many say it was Jackson's finest hour: Without bloodshed or war, by means of adroit diplomacy including both credible threats and tangible rewards, he'd steered the nation through its first constitutional crisis. Jackson knew, though, the truce was unstable. He made a prediction. One day, South Carolina would again try to destroy the Union by nullifying a law. Next time, he said, the issue would be slavery.

Jackson was then at the height of his popularity. In June, he set out on a Northern tour, traveling by stagecoach from Baltimore to Philadelphia and then on to New York and Boston. Everywhere he went he was met with parades, toasts, and accolades. In Boston, thousands of children lined the streets, their parents behind them. Harvard gave him an honorary degree. The crowds thrilled Jackson—and terrified his political enemies, who believed Jackson was accumulating a dangerous amount of power.

* * * * * * * * * * * * * * *

Jackson next turned his attention to the Second Bank of the United States. To destroy the bank once and for all, Jackson decided to move all federal deposits to various state banks. His critics called the plan foolish: There were no federal government controls over the state banks, so the funds would not be secure.

But Jackson was determined. He ordered his Treasury secretary, William Duane, to remove the funds. Duane refused, so Jackson fired him and replaced him with one of his Kitchen Cabinet members, Roger Taney. Taney moved the funds to state banks.

Congress pounced, accusing Jackson of overreaching: Nothing gave him the authority to move federal funds. Such authority rested with the Congress. Jackson disagreed on the grounds that he had won an election with a clear majority, and that the driving issue in the election was the bank. Therefore he claimed to be acting at the command of the people to protect them from Biddle and the national bank.

Biddle struck back. He recalled all federal loans, demanding immediate payment in specie, or hard coins. With fewer coins in circulation, and borrowers defaulting because many lacked the cash to immediately repay their loans, the nation experienced its second financial panic.

The Senate was enraged with Jackson for overstepping congressional authority and moving the funds, and voted to censure him for illegal orders. Pressure mounted on Jackson to back down and replace the funds, but he refused. He called Biddle's tactics of recalling loans bullying, and he declared that he would not be bullied.

Biddle and Jackson were locked in a dangerous rivalry: If neither backed down, the nation's economy would be smashed. "The bank, Mr. Van Buren, is trying to kill me," Jackson said. "But I will kill it."

Seeing that Jackson wasn't about to budge, Biddle gave in, restoring the flow of credit. Jackson still would not relent until what he considered the monster was dead. In April of 1834, the House of Representatives upheld Jackson's veto against renewing the bank's charter. The bank was shut down. Jackson used the remaining funds to pay off the national debt. He was the first—and last—president to pay off the national debt, a feat he accomplished by liquidating the bank and slashing all government spending, including highways, bridges, canals, and any infrastructure.

Jackson was jubilant. It had taken him so many years to repay his own debt after the land-sale fiasco, he had come to believe debt of any kind was a moral failing. He thus considered his act of paying off the national debt his gift to the nation.

✶ ✶ ✶ ✶ ✶ ✶ ✶ ✶ ✶ ✶ ✶ ✶ ✶ ✶ ✶

A political movement arose to fight against Jackson. A new party formed, calling itself the Whigs, a name chosen to evoke the group who had opposed the monarchy in England. People joined who were upset by Jackson's brutal treatment of the Indians. Others joined because of Jackson's unrepentant slave ownership. Some joined because they were pro-business and pro-banking. Still others joined because they thought Jackson was vindictive and ignorant and they were terrified of the direction he was taking the country. People joined for such different reasons, there wasn't much to hold the party together as a group—except dislike of Andrew Jackson.

Whig headquarters, 1840. Artist unknown.

Among those who joined the Whig party was a twenty-five-year-old man who was then serving as the postmaster of New Salem, Illinois, and deputy county surveyor. His name was Abraham Lincoln.

One cold damp day in January in 1835, Jackson, who was then sixty-seven years old, attended a memorial service in the Capitol for South Carolina congressman Warren Davis. Jackson emerged from the building leaning on his walking stick and the arm of his Treasury secretary, Levi Woodbury. As he stepped into the pale sunlight, he came face-to-face with a man named Richard Lawrence, a house painter convinced that he was the unrecognized heir to the British throne and that the United States government owed him an enormous sum of gold.

Lawrence pulled a single-shot pistol from under his cloak. He pointed it at Jackson's chest, and squeezed the trigger. The result was a loud crack, but nothing more; the gun had misfired.

Etching of the assassination attempt, 1835. Artist unknown.

All around was general panic and shrieks. Jackson might have been growing feeble, but he hadn't lost any of his fighting spirit. Instantly he lunged at his would-be assassin, brandishing his walking stick like a truncheon. The gunman pulled out a second pistol and aimed again—this time almost at point-blank range. He squeezed the trigger, but again misfired. A congressman wrestled the gunman to the floor and got his guns away from him.

Later the guns were examined and found to be properly loaded. The chances of two properly loaded pistols misfiring have been calculated to be one in one hundred and twenty-five thousand. Experts have concluded that the dampness of the weather saved Jackson's life by preventing the powder from igniting.

Jackson thus became the first American president to be the target of an assassin.

Jackson became convinced that the attacker was part of a larger plot to bring him down and destroy his presidency. The New York *Evening Post* saw the attack as a symbol of the passions, including fear and anger, that Jackson aroused. The truth was more mundane: The attacker was simply unhinged. He was confined to a hospital for the insane, where he died in 1861.

Nullification

Through most of his presidency, Jackson was able to ignore the abolitionists, who he viewed as a minority group out to make trouble. In fact, he considered the nullifiers and the abolitionists to be two heads of the same monster, both rabble-rousers out to destroy the Union. When in 1835 the American Anti-Slavery Society began flooding the South with anti-slavery flyers sent through the U.S. Postal Service, Jackson could no longer ignore them.

Many Southerners were furious—and alarmed. Many lived in fear of slave uprisings, particularly in South Carolina, where slaves outnumbered whites. The bloodiest slave revolt of all time, Nat Turner's slave rebellion in Virginia, occurred seven months after the *Liberator*, an antislavery newspaper, began sending copies of the newspaper into the South. While there was no proof that there was a connection between the rebellion and the newspaper, many Southerners insisted there was. Like Jackson, many Southerners didn't believe the abolitionists were motivated by humanitarian impulses. They saw the abolitionists as part of an evil plot to massacre Southern whites by fomenting unrest and slave rebellion.

While Andrew Jackson and many in the South believed abolitionism was a Northern conspiracy to crush the South, in fact, there was a growing global movement against slavery. Mexico achieved its independence from Spain in 1819, and abolished slavery in 1829, causing tension among the American slave owners in what is now Texas but was then part of Mexico. In 1833, slavery was abolished in the British Empire. When the Virginia legislature considered the gradual emancipation of Virginia's slaves and seriously debated the issue, many in the Deep South were shocked. The measure in Virginia failed, but others across the South declared Virginia infested with Yankee influence.

To keep newspapers like the *Liberator* out of South Carolina, the state passed a ban on incendiary materials—anything that might incite anger and violence. When the American Anti-Slavery Association tracts began flooding into Charleston in 1835, postmaster Alfred Huger was alarmed. He had a duty to the federal government to deliver the mail *and* a duty to obey South Carolina law. He contacted Amos Kendall, formerly a member of Jackson's Kitchen Cabinet and now U.S. postmaster general, to find out what he should do. Kendall turned to Jackson for advice.

First, Jackson suggested delivering the materials only to people who subscribed—a tiny number in Charleston. Next, he had the idea of publicly shaming the people who did subscribe by publishing their names. Recognizing problems with both of these ideas, Kendall ignored the advice and instead let the local post offices in South Carolina decide what to do. The post offices in South Carolina simply failed to deliver the tracts.

Jackson called for a new federal law that would ban mail going into Southern states that was intended to incite slaves to rebel—a law that would have allowed for federal censorship of the mail. His proposal drew sharp criticism from both sides. The liberals in the North were horrified over the very idea of the federal government censoring mail. Calhoun and others who were pro-states' rights and pro-slavery denounced Jackson's proposed law as too soft on the Northern instigators.

In July 1836, Congress responded to the problem by passing a postal law upholding the government's commitment to deliver mail without censoring the contents. But Southern officials and post offices simply ignored the laws, and Jackson and his administration pretended not to notice.

* * * * * * * * * * * * * * *

The power to appoint Supreme Court justices means that a president's influence can last long after he leaves office. This was particularly true of Jackson, who, during the course of his eight years as president, was able to appoint six Supreme Court justices, including Roger Taney, a member of the Kitchen Cabinet, who replaced John Marshall as Chief Justice and held militant pro-slavery and pro–states' rights positions.

As Jackson's second term drew to a close, one task remained: to help his vice president Martin Van Buren become elected as the next president of the United States. Jackson worked hard, throwing his fighting spirit into the campaign. Van Buren ran on Jackson's popularity. The Whigs nominated three candidates, thus dividing the anti–Jackson and Van Buren vote. On December 7, 1836, Martin Van Buren was elected eighth president of the United States by a slim margin, winning 51 percent of the popular vote.

Van Buren was inaugurated on a sunny and brisk Saturday in March. Unlike Jackson's first inauguration eight years earlier, this was a well-orchestrated affair, as much a tribute to Jackson as the outgoing president as a celebration of the incoming Van Buren. For the first time, the incoming and outgoing presidents rode together to the Capitol. In his inaugural address, Van Buren pledged to walk in the footsteps of Andrew Jackson.

Roger Taney administered Van Buren's oath of office. Jackson had good reason to feel his legacy was secure. His vice president and personal choice was succeeding him. His good friend Roger Taney was now the Chief Justice of the Supreme Court, and five other justices he had chosen sat on the Court. In his words, the only thing he had left to do was to return to the Hermitage, "set my house in order, and go to sleep alongside my dear departed wife."

14

Legacy

"When I review the arduous administration through which I have passed, the formidable opposition I have met to its very close by the combined talents, wealth, and power of the whole aristocracy of the Union, aided as they were by the money monopoly, the US Bank, with its power of corruption . . . the result must be not only pleasing to me, but to every patriot."

—Andrew Jackson

The year after Jackson left office, the American economy fell into chaos. With each state bank issuing its own notes, and many printing massive amounts of money—making exactly the same mistakes that had led to the panic in 1819—there was another crash, this one marking the start of the longest depression in United States history, lasting six full years. Jackson's enemies blamed the economic crisis on a vindictive, foolhardy, and ignorant president. Jackson, though, from retirement at the Hermitage, disagreed.

The problem, he claimed, was using paper money and bank notes instead of gold. No wonder the value fluctuated wildly, he said, when paper was worthless.

Hannah, the slave who cared for both Rachel and Andrew Jackson. Photographer unknown.

Jackson lived his last years quietly at the Hermitage, sick and in pain, cared for by Hannah, the slave who had been with the Jacksons since she was a toddler and who had cared for Rachel during her final illness. When the word spread that Jackson was dying, a steady stream of visitors and well-wishers flocked to the Hermitage. Perfect strangers came because they wanted to say they had met Andrew Jackson.

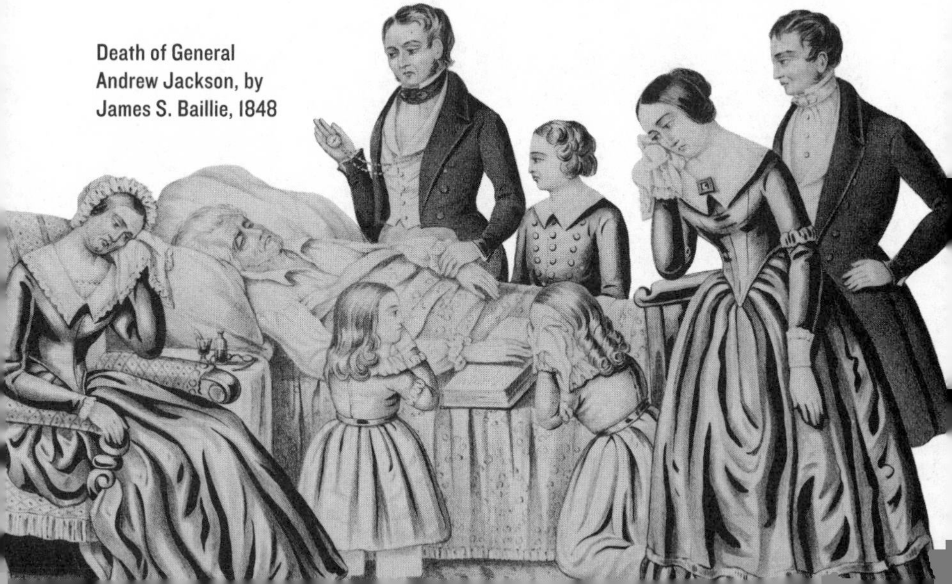

Death of General Andrew Jackson, by James S. Baillie, 1848

The Hermitage showing the dome over the tombs of both Rachel and Andrew Jackson. During Jackson's presidency, beginning in 1831, he made extensive additions to the original Hermitage home, adding one story to both sides of the house, with a dining room, pantry, and library. Later he transformed the front, increased the ceiling heights, and added decorative features to the façade. Image created March 29, 1856.

Legacy

On June 8, 1845, when he was seventy-eight years old, Jackson died peacefully in his bed, surrounded by his family. His last words were those of a patriarch: “Oh do not cry—be good children and we will all meet in heaven.” Two days later, he was buried in the garden at the Hermitage next to Rachel.

A towering figure, Jackson dominated his age. He created the nation's first populist movement and transformed Jefferson's Democratic-Republicans into a grass roots political party. Presidents ever since Jackson have followed his example of vetoing whatever laws they don't like. This means that before writing and proposing legislation, Congress must first consider what the president will do. With the simple weapon of the veto, Jackson moved the seat of power from Congress to the White House.

By facing down South Carolina and declaring nullification unconstitutional, and by strengthening the office of the presidency—and by shattering the notion that a president must be born into a pedigreed family or receive a certain kind of education—Jackson paved the way for Abraham Lincoln.

While Jackson did not succeed in completely turning the republic into a democracy, the Jacksonian era can be viewed as a movement from what has been called Jeffersonian Democracy—power in the hands of the ruling elite—to a more egalitarian democracy giving voice to common people. While federal judges are still appointed for life, many states changed their own constitutions to allow judges in state courts to be selected by voters in regular elections. Moreover, the election of 1828 marked a new era in national politics with campaigns reaching out to ordinary voters, often with stirring rhetoric. The form of democracy Jackson advocated—and to some extent brought about—has come to be called Jacksonian Democracy.

Jackson's watchword and campaign battle cry was "Reform!" but he embraced a backward-looking vision, a pining for an America that existed before the Industrial Revolution—a simpler America where personal liberty (for white men) was paramount.

On the surface, the America of today doesn't have much in common with the America of Jackson's vision. America's economy is no longer agrarian. There is a new national bank called the Federal Reserve, much more tightly regulated than the previous national banks. There is no longer a gold standard. State governments no longer have unfettered freedom in how they treat people living within their borders. But Jackson's brand of conservatism—including his nationalism and notions of white male supremacy—threads its way through American history from his time to ours, and remains a powerful force in our politics.

Notes

Prologue: A Mob in the White House

2 "Fellow citizens . . . be worth defending": Jackson's First Inaugural Address, avalon.law.yale.edu/19th_century/jackson1.asp.

3 "The majesty of the people . . . most vulgar and gross in the nation": Perley's Reminiscences of Sixty Years in the National Metropolis, 92–96 and Margaret B. Smith, The First Forty Years of Washington Society, 283 as quoted by Remini, *Andrew Jackson*, p. 120.

1. A Brutal Boyhood

5 "It is very true . . . fabrick of free government": Jackson to Samuel Swartwout, February 22, 1825, Papers of Andrew Jackson, Rotunda, vol. 6.

5 didn't care which colony their home was in: Jackson believed he was born in South Carolina. Recent scholarship, however, suggests that he was born in a relative's home on the North Carolina side of the border. See, for example, Booream, 11–12.

8 "a set of the most lowest vilest crew breathing": *Hooker*, 14.

9 "poor mind indeed which can't think of at least two ways to spell a word": Widely attributed to Andrew Jackson; source unknown.

9 "I could throw him three . . . never would give up.": Remini, vol. 1, 9. Slightly different versions, with slightly different wording, are given in earlier biographies.

9 "By God, if any of you laughs, I'll kill him": Parton, *The Life of Andrew Jackson*, 64, as quoted by Remini, vol. 1, 9.

11 "from the ferocious attacks": Booream, 248, note 7

13 "Passed through the Waxhaws . . . I could have shot him." Jackson's

Description of His Experiences, Papers of Andrew Jackson, Rotunda, vol. 1.

15 "Who goes there?": Booream, 86.

17 "I am a prisoner of war and claim to be treated as such": Booream, 97. This story first appeared in *The Life of Andrew Jackson*, by Reid and Eaton, 12–13, published in 1817. The book is so rare that even the Library of Congress does not have an undamaged copy.

18 "as soon as our relationship was known . . . no regard was paid to them": Jackson's Description of His Experiences, Papers of Andrew Jackson, Rotunda, vol. 1.

19 "Being anxious to see the battle . . . an aperture about an inch in diameter": Jackson's Description of his Experiences, Papers of Andrew Jackson, Rotunda, vol. 1.

19 "Never were hearts eleated more than ours at the glitter of the americans swords": Jackson's Description of his Experiences, Papers of Andrew Jackson, Rotunda, vol. 1.

20 "The fury of a violent storm . . . next day I was dangerously ill": Jackson's Description of his Experiences, Papers of Andrew Jackson, Rotunda, vol. 1.

21 "Make friends by being . . . settle them cases yourself": These words are engraved on a memorial marking a place near where Betty Jackson died in Lancaster County, South Carolina.

2. Head of All the Rowdies

24 "[B]rought up under the tyranny of Britain . . . the mild administration of a republican government": Andrew Jackson to Willie Blount, January 4, 1813, cdn.loc.gov/service/mss/maj/01010/01010_0291_0292.pdf.

26 "many other such men . . . spent money rather too freely": Booream, 122.

30 "What! . . . if Andrew Jackson can be president, anybody can!": Remini, Robert V. *Andrew Jackson*. Harper Collins 1999.

30 "Andrew Jackson . . . mischievous fellow that ever lived in Salisbury": Parton, vol. 1, 104, as quoted by Remini, vol. 1, 29–30.

30 "head of all the rowdies hereabouts": Parton, vol. 1, 104–105, as quoted by Booream, 157.

3. Romance on the Frontier

34 "With what pleasing hopes . . . during this transitory and fluctuating life": Jackson to Rachel, May 9, 1796, Papers of Andrew Jackson, Rotunda, vol 1.

35 "about eighteen or twenty years of age": Record of Slave Sale, November 17, 1788, Papers of Andrew Jackson, Rotunda, vol. 1.

36–38 "When amans feelings . . . after court adjourned": Papers of Andrew Jackson, Rotunda, vol. 1.

41 "rippling with smiles and dimples": Davis, Burke, *Old Hickory*, 17, as quoted by Marrin, 47.

42 respect for the law, Jackson style, had arrived in Nashville: Remini, vol. 2, 21.

46 Sometime within the year . . .: The version I am following was recounted in *The Robards-Jackson Backcountry Scandal* by Ann Toplovich, reflecting the most recent scholarship on what actually occurred between Jackson, Robards, and Rachel. For a fuller account of what happened—and a convincing argument that accounts often given in many biographies are untrue, see Remini, vol. 2, 44, 57–67.

48 A common-law marriage is one in which the couple live together for a period of time and hold themselves out to friends, family, and the community as being married, but never go through a formal ceremony. Even today, a number of states recognize common-law marriages as legal, provided certain requirements are met.

4. Congressman Jackson

49 "[M]ischief springs from the power . . . employed altogether for their benefit": From Jackson's Farewell Address, March 4, 1837, available here: www.presidency.ucsb.edu/ws/?pid=67087.

53 "would be a gross violation of the fundamental laws of nature and of that distributive justice which is the glory of a nation": Tim Alan Garrison, *The Legal Ideology of Removal* (Athens: University of Georgia Press, 2002), as quoted by Magliocca, 14.

53 "Some say humanity dictates it . . . murdering her innocent citizens": Jackson to John McKee, May 16, 1794, Papers of Andrew Jackson, Rotunda, vol. 1.

55–56 "When it was seen that war was waged . . . it was time to make resistance": Rives, p. 48.

5. Justice, Jackson Style

60 "I am of the opinion . . . happiness of the people": This quotation of Jackson's was mentioned in the dedication of the Lawrence H. Cooke County Courthouse. Dedication can be found here: www.congress.gov/congressional-record/1997/9/25/extensions-of-remarks-section.

60 "short, untechnical, unlearned, sometimes ungrammatical, and generally right": This quotation originates with Amos Kendall, a staunch supporter of Jackson, as quoted by Remini, vol. 1, 114.

60 "Do what is right between the parties. That is what the law always means": Marrin, 52.

63 "Now, surrender . . . it's about time to sing small, and so I did": Slightly different versions of this story can be found in the early biographies of Jackson. This version is from Parton, vol. 1, 227, as quoted by Remini, vol. 1, 115. A slightly different version can be found in a James McLaughlin's letter to Amos Kendall, January 3, 1843. See Remini, note 8, p. 441.

66 "Services? . . . *her* sacred name?": Parton, vol. 1, 164, as quoted by Remini, vol. 1, 121.

68 "affected no style, and put on no airs of greatness": Marrin, 62.

69 "negroes will complain without cause": Jackson to Andrew Jackson Jr. August 19, 1829. cdn.loc.gov/service/mss/maj/01073/01073_0280_0283.pdf.

71 "a handsome theatre for our enterprising young men and a source of acquiring fame": Jackson to James Winchester, October 4, 1806, Papers of Andrew Jackson, Rotunda, vol. 2.

72–73 "sacred . . . worthless scoundrel." Remini, 140.

73 "Great God! . . . Have I missed him?": This story is taken from Parton, *The Life of Andrew Jackson*, and Amos Kendall's accounts, as quoted by Remini, 142.

6. The Beat of the War Drum

75 "The hour of national vengeance is now at hand . . . the power of your arms": Jackson to the Second Division, March 7, 1812. Papers of Andrew Jackson, Rotunda, vol. 2.

78–79 "*Citizens! . . . Who are we? . . .* liberties and property which they dare call their own": Jackson to the Second Division, March 7, 1812. Papers of Andrew Jackson, Rotunda, vol. 2.

80 "Sir . . . dismissed from public service . . ." founders.archives.gov/documents/Madison/03-06-02-0116, footnote 3.

80 "Kiss my little Andrew for me and tell him his papa is coming home": Jackson to Rachel, March 15, 1813, available here: memory.loc.gov/service/mss/maj/01011/01011_0231_0232.pdf.

80 "act as a father to the sick and to the well": Jackson to Rachel, March 15, 1813, available here: memory.loc.gov/service/mss/maj/01011/01011_0231_0232.pdf.

83 "The health of your general . . . drenched in the blood of our fellow-citizens." Jackson to the Tennessee Volunteers,

September 24, 1813, Papers of Andrew Jackson, Rotunda, vol. 2.

84 "laying waste their villages, burning their houses, killing their warriors, and leading into captivity their wives and children": Frederick M. Binder, *The Color Problem in Early America as Viewed by John Adams, Jefferson, and Jackson* (Mouton: The Hague, 1968) as quoted by Marrin, 76.

84 "shot them like dogs": William C. Davis, *Three Roads to the Alamo: The Lives and Fortunes of David Crockett, James Bowie, and William Barret Travis.* (New York: Harper Collins, 1998) as quoted by Marrin, 76.

85 "when I reflect that he as to his relations . . . that fortune has thrown on my hands:" Jackson to Rachel, December 29, 1813, Papers of Andrew Jackson, Rotunda, vol. 2.

7. The Battle of New Orleans

91 "Some believe me . . . unconcern and careless indifference": Jackson to Samuel Swartwout, March 25, 1824, Papers of Andrew Jackson, Rotunda, vol. 2.

94 "a jug of whisky, a pack of cards, and a gun": Howe, 11.

94 "We have more dread . . . from open enemies": Jackson and Claiborne's correspondence, September 8, 1814, as quoted by Warshauer, 21.

94 "punished with the utmost severity": Jackson to Maj. Gen. Jacques P. Villere, Dec. 19, 1815, as quoted by Warshauer, 24.

96 "this ingenious symbol of a land of liberty": Parton, *The Life of Andrew Jackson*, II, 176, as quoted by Marrin, 96.

98 "the enemy are still hovering around us & perhaps mediates an attack": Warshauer, 32.

100 "His popularity is unbounded . . . speak of him with rapture": *Tennessee Gazette*, July 17, 1818, as quoted by Wilentz, location 712.

101 "the growing greatness of our nation": Jackson to James Monroe, June 2, 1818, Papers of Andrew Jackson, Rotunda, vol. 4.

8. The Corrupt Bargain

104 "John Quincy Adams . . . can fight": Marrin, 145.

105 "half naked women and men . . . any crime but being black": Howe, 129.

108 "fire bell in the night . . . I now doubt it much": Jefferson to William Short, April 13, 1820. Available here: rotunda.upress.virginia.edu /founders/default.xqy?keys=FOEA-print-04-02-02-1218.

111 "I am . . . a scalping knife in the other": Jackson to Maj. George W. Martin, January 2, 1824, as quoted by Remini, vol. 2, 60.

115 "He is one of the most unfit . . . a dangerous man": Howe, 205.

115 These numbers are from Howe, 208. Because not all states counted popular votes, the numbers are approximate, and different historians offer slightly different numbers.

117 "satisfy him . . . without any personal considerations for himself": Remini vol. 2, 89.

117 "give the strongest guarantee . . . republic to ruin": Wilentz, location 829.

117 Conclusions are those of historian Wilentz, location 834.

117–118 "This, to my mind . . . bartered for promise of office": Jackson to John Coffee, February 19, 1825, Papers of Andrew Jackson, Rotunda, vol. 6.

9. Demagogue or Passionate Patriot?

121 "Fear not . . . cannot be corrupted": Andrew Jackson to Van Buren, May 1, 1838. Van Buren Papers, Library of Congress.

122 "lighthouses in the sky," Remini, vol. 2, 111.

128 "I have great confidence . . . cannot fear the result": Jackson to

James Hamilton Jr., June 29, 1828, Papers of Andrew Jackson, Rotunda, vol. 6.

128 "secure to every man equal rights & privileges": Jackson to Andrew Jackson Donelson, April 11, 1824, Papers of Andrew Jackson, Rotunda, vol. 5.

129 "the people of New England . . . keep down the South and West": Remini vol. 3, 15.

136–137 "General Jackson's mother . . . General JACKSON is one": Marrin, 154.

138 Jackson won with 56 percent of the popular vote and 68 percent of the electoral college: The population of the United States at the time was nearly thirteen million. The number of voters was 1,155,340.

139 "I assure you . . . palace at Washington": Remini, vol. 2, 149.

140 "I shall never forget his look of grief"; Parton, *The Life of Andrew Jackson*, vol. 3, 161.

140 "A being so . . . could not dishonor": www.whitehouse.gov/1600/first-ladies/racheljackson.

10. The Indian Removal Act

142 "It will be my sincere and constant desire . . . feelings of our people": First inauguaral address of Andrew Jackson, available here: avalon.law.yale.edu/19th_century/jackson1.asp.

144 "we are getting on here . . . rats who have been plundering the Treasury": Andrew Jackson to John McLemore, April 1828; lcweb2.loc.gov/service/mss/maj/06161/06161_0133_0136.pdf.

145 "not be in accordance . . . credit of the administration." Van Buren to Andrew Jackson, April 23, 1829, as quoted by Remini, vol. 2, 198.

145 "is more like a son . . . grateful heart": Jackson to Rachel, February 27, 1824, as quoted by Remini, vol. 2, 161.

146 "His wife is held . . . into society": Meacham, location 1507.

149 "Two gold . . . treasures of the earth to use": www.georgiaencyclopedia.org/articles/history-archaeology/gold-rush.

149 "Our neighbors . . . we are an abused people": Transcription from the Cherokee Phoenix available here: www.wcu.edu/library/DigitalCollections/CherokeePhoenix/Vol2/no08/pg2col4.htm.

152 "red children . . . It will be yours forever": Proceedings of the Indian Board in the City of New York, 5.

153 "his body shook; his voice cracked": Remini, vol. 2, 207.

155–156 "Now is the time . . . defenseless people from ruin . . . living monuments of the white man's wrongs:" Maglioca, 25.

157 "The road is filled with the sick": Jahoda, *The Trail of Tears*, San Antonio, Texas: Wings Books, 1975, 87, as quoted by Marrin, 222.

157 "To see a remnant . . . move the stoutest heart": Jahoda, *The Trail of Tears*, 153–155, as quoted by Marrin, 222.

11. Who Decides?

158 "government being instituted . . . is necessarily subordinate to them": Jackson to Joseph Desha, June 25, 1825, Papers of Andrew Jackson, Rotunda, vol. 6.

160 "this disgusting petticoat business": Samuel D. Ingham to Samuel McKean, February 25, 1831, as quoted by Meacham, p. 172.

166 "our country will be like a bag of meal . . . will run out": Remini, vol. 3, 16.

166–167 "Our union . . . most dear": From Martin Van Buren, *The Autobiography of Martin Van Buren*. United States Printing Office, 1920, 416, as quoted by Meacham, p. 135.

167 "repugnant to the Constitution": *Worcester v. Georgia,* 31 U.S. 513 (1832).

170 "All I want in . . . in the Cherokee nation": Jahoda, *The Trail of Tears*, 224, as quoted by Marrin, 229.

12. Jackson's War with the Bank

171 "[Y]ou know my . . . if even the constitution would permit it": Jackson to William Berkeley Lewis, July 16, 1820, Papers of Andrew Jackson, Rotunda, vol. 4.

171 "It gives me pleasure . . . approaching to a happy consummation": The part of Jackson's message concerning the removal of the Indians can be found here: www.ourdocuments.gov /doc.php?flash=false&doc=25&page=transcript.

173 "No officer of the government . . . concerns of the bank": Biddle to Thomas Swann, March 17, 1824, as quoted by Willitz, location 1291.

176 "to make sure it would reach the ears of the President": Willitz, location 1344.

179 "carry themselves back . . . spirit manifested in the debates": Thomas Jefferson to William Johnson, June 12, 1823, available here: founders.archives.gov/documents/Jefferson/98-01-02-3562.

179 "necessary and proper": *McCulloch v. Maryland*, 17 U.S. 316 (1819).

13. Nullification

181 "I draw a wide difference . . . acts unauthorized in it": Jackson to Robert Hayne, February 6, 1831, as quoted by Remini, vol. 2, 332–333.

184 "reduces everything to anarchy & strikes at the very existence of society": Jackson to Maunsel White, December 22, 1832, as quoted by Remini, vol. 3, 22.

184 "if the sacred soil of Carolina should be polluted by the footsteps of the invader": Remini, vol. 3, 14.

185 "if one drop of blood . . . really hang anybody, do you?": Howe, 406.

188 "The bank . . . I will kill it": Martin Van Buren, *The Autobiography of Martin Van Buren*, vol. 2, 625, as quoted by Willitz, location 1352.

197 "set my house in order, and go to sleep alongside my dear departed

wife": Jackson to Reverend Hardy M. Cryer, June 17, 1832, as quoted by Remini, vol. 2, 375.

14. Legacy

198 "When I review the arduous . . . every patriot": Jackson to President Van Buren, March 30, 1837; www.loc.gov/resource/maj.01098_0254_0259/?st=text.

201 "Oh do not cry—be good children and we will all meet in heaven": Meacham, p. 345.

Backmatter

220–223 Jackson's bank veto is available here: avalon.law.yale.edu/19th_century/ajveto01.asp.

Time Line

March 15, 1767 ✶ Jackson is born in the Waxhaws community.

April 11, 1781 ✶ Jackson and his brother Robert are arrested by the British and taken to Camden Jail.

April 28, 1791 ✶ Jackson and his brother are released from jail in a prisoner exchange; returned home.

June 1791 ✶ Betty Jackson dies.

1786 ✶ Jackson moves to Salisbury to study law.

1788 ✶ John McNairy, Jackson, and others travel to Tennessee, where Jackson takes up his post as prosecuting attorney; fights duel with Waightstill Avery.

1790 ✶ Jackson "marries" Rachel Donelson.

1796 ✶ Jackson participates in the Tennessee Constitutional Convention and is elected to the U.S. House of Representatives.

1797 ✶ Jackson is elected to the U.S. Senate.

1798 ✶ Jackson resigns his Senate seat; is elected judge of the Tennessee Superior Court.

1802 ✶ Jackson is appointed major general of the Tennessee militia.

1805–1807 ✶ Jackson becomes involved in the Burr conspiracy.

1812 ✶ Jackson leads troops to Natchez; earns the nickname Old Hickory.

1813 ✶ Jackson fights with Jesse and Thomas Hart Benton; he leads troops against the Muscogees. Rescues and adopts Lyncoya.

Time Line

1814 ✶ Jackson orders the execution of John Woods; defeats Muscogees at Horseshoe Bend.

1814 ✶ President Monroe commissions Jackson as major general in the U.S. Army.

1815 ✶ Jackson leads the Americans to defeat the British in the Battle of New Orleans.

1818 ✶ Jackson invades Spanish Florida; captures Pensacola.

1822 ✶ The Tennessee legislature nominates Jackson for president, then elects him to the Senate.

1824 ✶ Jackson receives a plurality of the popular vote in the presidential election.

1825 ✶ Jackson is defeated for president in the U.S. House of Representatives; resigns his Senate seat; is nominated for president by Tennessee's legislature.

1828 ✶ Jackson is elected president.

May 28, 1829 ✶ Congress passes the Indian Removal Act.

1832 ✶ Jackson vetoes the Bank Renewal Bill.

December 5, 1832 ✶ Jackson is reelected.

March 1833 ✶ Jackson faces down the nullifiers of South Carolina.

1835 ✶ Assassination is attempted on Andrew Jackson.

March 1, 1836 ✶ The Second Bank of the United States expires and goes out of existence.

December 7, 1836 ✶ Martin Van Buren is elected president with 51 percent of the popular vote and 170 votes in the electoral college.

June 8, 1945 ✶ Jackson dies at home.

Selected Writings of Andrew Jackson

TO RACHEL JACKSON, FROM KNOXVILLE, MAY 9, 1796

My Dearest Heart

It is with the greate pleasure I sit down to write you. Tho I am absent My heart rests with you. With what pleasing hopes I view the future period when I shall be restored to your arms there to spend My days in Domestic Sweetness with you the Dear Companion of my life, never to be separated from you again during this Transitory and fluctuating life.

I mean to retire from the Buss of publick life, and Spend My Time with you alone in Sweet Retirement, which is My only ambition and ultimate wish.

I have this moment finished My business here which I have got in good Train and hope to wind it up this Tauer, and will leave this tomorrow Morning for Jonesborough where I hope to finish it, and tho it is now half after ten o'clock, could not think of going to bed without writing you. May it give you pleasure to Receive it. May it add to your Contentment until I return. May you be blessed with health. May the Goddess of Slumber every evening light on your eyebrows and gently lull you to sleep, and conduct you through the night with pleasing thoughts and pleasant dreams. Could I only know you were contented and enjoyed Peace of Mind, what satisfaction it woould afford me whilst travelling the loanly and tiresome road. It would relieve My anxious breast and shorten the way—May the great "I am" bless and protect you until that happy and wished for moment arrives when I am restored to your sweet embrace which is the Nightly prayer of your affectionate husband,

Andrew Jackson.

P. S. My compliments to my good old Mother Mrs. Donelson, that best of friends. Tell her with what pain I reflect upon leaving home without shaking her by the hand and asking her blessing.

A.J.

LETTER TO JOHN OVERTON AFTER THE VOTING IN 1824

My Dear friend

I have recd your kind letter of the 28th Ult, & perused it with attention—You will find from the public Journals before this reaches you, that the Electoral vote of Louisiana is not for Mr Clay, & of course he does not go into the House, as the third highest—what May be the result of the vote by the House of Representatives I know not—I hope my friends will continue to take principle for their guide; and let me rise or fall upon the rule that the people have the right to choose the chief executive of the nation, and a majority of their voices have a right to govern, agreable to the declared principles of the constitution—

Having been supported by the majority of the people, I can have no feelings on the occasion—If party or intrigue should prevail, and exclude me, I shall retire to my comfortable farm with great pleasure—there you know; was the hight of my ambition, there is the only contentment for me, there I could in retirement mingle with my sincere friends. 'in rural retirement' should I be selected to preside over the destinies of this great & growing nation—my best Judgt shall be employed for its prosperity &

happiness; I am aware of the responsibility of the station—& with my own consent I should never aspired to the responsibility—but, let the lords will be done—and if placed in the Executive chair, I shall endeavour, with an honest zeal to discharge the duties of that station & bring to my aid as far as I can command it, the best Talents & Virtue of this nation.

Mrs. Jackson has stood the Journey well, is in good health– and anxious to hear from our little Andrews—
will you have the goodness when you are in Nashville to present us to The Revd. Mr Campbell, & Mr J. C McLamore & request of them from me to give us the information of their situation & health—

Mrs. J. Joins me in best wishes for your & Mrs. O. health & happiness, and believe me your friend—

Andrew Jackson

EXCERPTS FROM JACKSON'S BANK VETO

WASHINGTON, July 10, 1832.

To the Senate.

A bank of the United States is in many respects convenient for the Government and useful to the people. Entertaining this opinion, and deeply impressed with the belief that some of the powers and privileges possessed by the existing bank are unauthorized by the Constitution, subversive of the rights of the States, and dangerous to the liberties of the people, I felt it my duty at an early period of my Administration to call the attention of Congress to the practicability of organizing an institution combining all its advantages and obviating these objections. I sincerely regret that in the act before me I can perceive none of those modifications of the bank charter which are necessary, in my opinion, to make it compatible with justice, with sound policy, or with the Constitution of our country.

The present corporate body . . . enjoys an exclusive privilege of banking under the authority of the General Government, a monopoly of its favor and support, and, as a necessary consequence, almost a monopoly of the foreign and domestic exchange. The powers, privileges, and favors bestowed upon it in the original charter, by increasing the value of the stock far above its par value, operated as a gratuity of many millions to the stockholders . . .

Every monopoly and all exclusive privileges are granted at the expense of the public, which ought to receive a fair equivalent. The many millions which this act proposes to bestow on the stockholders of the existing bank must come directly or indirectly out of the earnings of the American people. It is due to them, therefore, if their Government sell monopolies and exclusive privileges, that they should at least exact for them as much as they are worth in open market. The value of the monopoly in this case May be correctly ascertained. The twenty-eight millions of stock would probably be at an advance of 50 per cent, and command in market at least $42,000,000, subject to the payment of the present bonus. The present value of the monopoly, therefore, is $17,000,000, and this the act proposes to sell for three millions, payable in fifteen annual installments of $200,000 each.

It is not conceivable how the present stockholders can have any claim to the special favor of the Government. The present corporation has enjoyed its monopoly during the period stipulated in the original contract. If we must have such a corporation, why should not the Government sell out the whole stock and thus secure to the people the full market value of the privileges granted? Why should not Congress create and sell twenty-eight millions of stock, incorporating the purchasers with all the powers and privileges secured in this act and putting the premium upon the sales into the Treasury?

. . . I have now done my duty to my country. If sustained by my fellow citizens, I shall be grateful and happy; if not, I shall find in the motives which impel me ample grounds for contentment and peace. In the difficulties which surround us and the dangers which threaten our institutions there is cause for neither disMay nor alarm. For relief and deliverance let us firmly rely on that kind Providence which I am sure watches with peculiar care over the destinies of our Republic, and on the intelligence and wisdom of our countrymen. Through His abundant goodness and heir patriotic devotion our liberty and Union will be preserved.

"The Hunters of Kentucky"

This is an excerpt from a song written by Samuel Woodworth in 1821, commemorating the Battle of New Orleans, sometimes called "Half Horse and Half Alligator."

Ye gentlemen and ladies fair
Who grace this famous city
Just listen, if you've time to spare
While I rehearse a ditty;
And for the opportunity
Conceive yourselves quite lucky
For 'tis not often that you see
A hunter from Kentucky!

Oh Kentucky, the hunters of Kentucky!
Oh Kentucky, the hunters of Kentucky!

We are a hardy, free-born race
Each man to fear a stranger;
Whate'er the game, we join in chase
Despising toil and danger
And if a daring foe annoys
Whate'er his strength and forces
We'll show him that Kentucky boys
Are alligator horses.

"The Hunters of Kentucky"

Oh Kentucky, the hunters of Kentucky!
Oh Kentucky, the hunters of Kentucky!

I s'pose you've read it in the prints
How Packenham attempted
To make old Hickory Jackson wince
But soon his scheme repented;
For we, with rifles ready cock'd
Thought such occasion lucky
And soon around the gen'ral flock'd
The hunters of Kentucky.

Oh Kentucky, the hunters of Kentucky!
Oh Kentucky, the hunters of Kentucky!

But Jackson he was wide awake
And was not scar'd at trifles
For well he knew what aim we take
With our Kentucky rifles:
So he led us down by Cypress swamp

The ground was low and mucky;
There stood John Bull in martial pomp
And here was old Kentucky

Oh Kentucky, the hunters of Kentucky!
Oh Kentucky, the hunters of Kentucky!

A bank was rais'd to hide our breasts
Not that we thought of dying
But that we always like to rest
Unless the game is flying
Behind it stood our little force

None wished it to be greater
For ev'ry man was half a horse
And half an alligator

Oh Kentucky, the hunters of Kentucky!
Oh Kentucky, the hunters of Kentucky!

They did not let our patience tire
Before they show'd their faces;
We did not choose to waste our fire
So snugly kept our places
But when so near we saw them wink
We thought it time to stop 'em
And 'twould have done you good, I think
To see Kentuckians drop 'em

Oh Kentucky, the hunters of Kentucky!
Oh Kentucky, the hunters of Kentucky!

The British found, 'twas vain to fight
Where lead was all their booty
And so they wisely took to flight
And left us all the beauty
And now, if danger e'er annoys
Remember what our trade is;
Just send for us Kentucky boys
And we'll protect ye, ladies.

Bibliography

Writing a biography of Andrew Jackson presents a special challenge: Sorting out the truth from the myth and folklore. Professor Hendrik Booream, in an appendix of *Young Hickory*, explains that some of the false information about Andrew Jackson's life stems from the nineteenth-century biography of Andrew Jackson written by Augustus Buell (1847–1904), who evidently invented anecdotes and quotations out of whole cloth to add color to his narrative. Many of these anecdotes were repeated by twentieth-century biographers and have come to be accepted as fact. Other stories were made up for political purposes; for example, the story invented by Jackson's supporters about how Jackson and Rachel were tricked into believing Rachel's husband has secured a divorce—a story still given in modern biographies as fact. Moreover, during heated presidential elections, both sides are likely to invent outright lies and slanders, which tend to get repeated and ultimately can be passed down as truth. Thus a reader can study two different biographies of Andrew Jackson and come away with two entirely different sets of facts.

Online Sources

Andrew Jackson Papers Collection, Library of Congress. Includes correspondence, memoranda, journals, speeches, and military records: www.loc.gov/collections/andrew-jackson-papers.

"Message to Congress on Indian Removal." The transcript of Jackson's message to Congress can be found here: www.ourdocuments.gov/doc.php?flash=false&doc=25&page=transcript.

National Archives, Founders Online, contains documents and letters from the Founding Fathers: founders.archives.gov.

New Georgia Encyclopedia, www.georgiaencyclopedia.org/articles/history-archaeology/gold-rush.

Papers of Andrew Jackson. Can be found as part of the Yale Law School Avalon Project: avalon.law.yale.edu/subject_menus/jackpap.asp.

Papers of Andrew Jackson digital edition, Daniel Feller, editor. Charlottesville: The University of Virginia Press, Rotunda, 2015–. This is a subscription service, available online and at many libraries: thepapersofandrewjackson.utk.edu/?page_id=1.

Parton, James. *Life of Andrew Jackson in Three Volumes.* New York: Mason Brothers, 1860. vol. 3 availble here: archive.org/details/lifeandrewjacks00partgoog.

Poore, Benjamin Perley. Perley's Reminiscences of Sixty Years in the National Metropolis. Published in 1886 and available here: archive.org/details/perleysreminisce00poor.

Rives, John C. *Abridgment of the Debates of Congress, from 1789 to 1856.* New York: Appleton and Company, 1857, available here: archive.org/details/abridgmentofdeba06unitiala.

Books and Articles

Booream, Hendrik. *Young Hickory: The Making of Andrew Jackson.* Dallas, Texas: Taylor Trade Publishing, 2001.

Eaton, Henry and John Reid. *The Life of Andrew Jackson: Major-General in the Service of the United States, Comprising a History of the War in the South, from the Commencement of the Creek Campaign to the Termination of the Hostilities before New Orleans.* Philadelphia: Samuel F. Bradford, 1824.

Feller, Daniel. *The Jacksonian Promise: America, 1815–1840.* Baltimore: Johns Hopkins Press, 1995.

Hooker, Richard. *The Carolina Backcountry on the Eve of the Revolution.* Chapel Hill, NC: University of North Carolina Press, 1953.

Howe, Daniel Walker. *What God Hath Wrought: The Transformation of America, 1815–1848*. New York: Oxford University Press, 2007.

Magliocca, Gerard N. *Andrew Jackson and the Constitution: The Rise and Fall of Generational Regimes*. Laurence, KS: University of Kansas Press, 2007.

Meacham, Jon. *American Lion: Andrew Jackson in the White House*. New York: Random House, 2008 (Kindle version).

Parsons, Lynn Hudson. *The Birth of Modern Politics: Andrew Jackson and the Election of 1828*. New York: Oxford University Press, 2009 (Kindle version).

Proceedings of the Indian Board in the City of New York: With Colonel McKenney's Address. New York: Vanderpool & Cole, Printers, 104 Beekman Street, 1829.

Remini, Robert. *Andrew Jackson and the Course of American Democracy, 17671821*, vol. 1. New York: Harper & Row, 1817.

———. *Andrew Jackson and the Course of American Democracy, 1822–1832*, vol. 2. New York: Harper & Row, 1817.

———. *Andrew Jackson and the Course of American Democracy, 1833–1845*, vol. 3. New York: Harper & Row, 1817.

Toplovich, Ann. "The Robards-Jackson Backcountry Scandal," muse.jhu.edu/article/572973.

Warshauer, Matthew, *Andrew Jackson and the Politics of Martial Law: Nationalism, Civil Liberties, and Partisanship*. Knoxville, TN: University of Tennessee Press, 2006.

Wilentz, Sean. *The Rise of American Democracy: Jefferson to Lincoln*. New York: Norton, 2005 (Kindle version).

Supreme Court Cases

McCulloch v. Maryland, 17 U.S. 316 (1819)

Worcester v. Georgia, 31 U.S. 513 (1832)

Acknowledgments

This book could not have been written without the unsung heroes of American historical preservation who have made reams of archival documents available to the public through online searches. These include the National Archives Online Records, the Yale Avalon Project, the Library of Congress, and the Papers of Andrew Jackson, digital edition, University of Virginia Press Rotunda. I owe a special thanks to Professor Daniel Feller, history professor at the University of Tennessee, Knoxville, and director of the Center for Jacksonian America, who patiently answered my questions and guided my research, helping me untangle the facts from the myths, folklore, and exaggerations. Any errors, of course, are my own.

The Abrams team once again turned a mere manuscript into a work of art: Howard Reeves, my editor; Chad Beckerman, designer; Amy Vreeland, managing editor; Masha Gunic, who saw this manuscript through each stage and offered constant support and help; Josh Berlowitz and Tom McNellis, who are amazing at catching errors; and Emily Daluga. Last but definitely not least, thanks to my first readers: Betsy Wattenberg, Carole Greeley, and Andy Schloss.

Index

Note: Page numbers in *italics* refer to illustrations.

Index